Copyright © 2023 by Trient Press

All rights reserved. No part of this publication may be reproduced, distributed, or transmitted in any form or by any means, including photocopying, recording, or other electronic or mechanical methods, without the prior written permission of the publisher, except in the case of brief quotations embodied in critical reviews and certain other noncommercial uses permitted by copyright law. For permission requests, write to the publisher, addressed "Attention: Permissions Coordinator," at the address below.

Criminal copyright infringement, including infringement without monetary gain, is investigated by the FBI and is punishable by up to five years in federal prison and a fine of $250,000.

Except for the original story material written by the author, all songs, song titles, and lyrics mentioned in the novel From Data to Disruption: How AI is Changing Business Forever are the exclusive property of the respective artists, songwriters, and copyright holder.

Trient Press
3375 S Rainbow Blvd
#81710, SMB 13135
Las Vegas,NV 89180

Ordering Information:
Quantity sales. Special discounts are available on quantity purchases by corporations, associations, and others. For details, contact the publisher at the address above.
Orders by U.S. trade bookstores and wholesalers. Please contact Trient Press: Tel: (775) 996-3844; or visit www.trientpress.com.

Printed in the United States of America

Publisher's Cataloging-in-Publication data
Trient Press
A title of a book : Trientrepreneur

PATH BENDER

BY: ANTONIO SMITH

Path Bender
Antonio T Smith Jr

Trient Press

AUTHOR TIPS: 06

- Autor Tips
- Maximizing Your Digital Footprint: Strategies for Authors in the Social Media Age
- Collaborative Writing in the Digital Era: Tools and Techniques for Success
- From Draft to Bestseller: Navigating the Publishing Process in 2024
- Balancing Creativity and Commerce: Pricing Strategies for Independent Authors
- The Art of Self-Promotion: Building Your Brand as an Author"

COVER FEATURE: Roosevelt Williams III: A Beacon of Community Empowerment and Peace in San Diego

TABLE OF CONTENTS
RIENTREPRENEUR
ISSUE 17

Editor-in-Chief
Head Staff-Writer
Melisa Ruscsak

Managing Editor
Graphic Design Editor
Kristina Wenzl-Figueroa

ECONOMICS SECTION:

- Global Economic Trends: Challenges and Opportunities in 2024
- Navigating Economic Uncertainty: Investment Strategies for Turbulent Times
- The Rise of Green Economics: How Sustainable Practices Are Shaping Markets
- Emerging Markets in 2024: Risks and Rewards for International Investors
- Trade Wars to Trade Wins: The Future of International Trade Agreements"

TECH SECTION: 51

- Artificial Intelligence in the Workplace: Enhancing Efficiency or Displacing Jobs?
- The Next Frontier: How Quantum Computing is Transforming Industries
- Blockchain Beyond Cryptocurrency: Diverse Applications in Business
- Cybersecurity in 2024: Protecting Your Business in the Digital Age
- The Impact of 5G Technology on Business Operations and Consumer Behavior

TRAVEL SECTION: 65

- Unveiling the Wonders of YBNB: A Journey to Remember
- Sycuan Resort: A Red Carpet Experience Amidst Serenity
- Exploring the Other Side of San Diego: A Quirky Guide to Fun-Filled Adventures
- Navigating the world: A Deaf Traveler's Perspective
- Unveiling the World of Dark Tourism: Exploring the Unconventional Side of Travel
- Recipes

Zoey's favorite childhood story is Orlana, the golden Faeryqueen. Oh her eigth birthday, her family takes her to Faery Tale Lnad where she meets her princess idol. Zoey's life changes dramatically. The nic lady she meets in the restroom is a trafficker who steals her away fro her family. Zoey grows u as hard-working slav until a hot line call opens up an investigation. Chance the attractive tutor assigned to work with her is, is suspicious o the family story.

Can Zoey trust him enough to open up her heart?

Is he the ray of hope she's been waiting for?

SHERI CHAPMAN

AUTHOR TIPS

TRIENT PRESS MAGAZINE — FEBRUARY/MARCH

Crafting Compelling Characters: Tips for Writers

Develop Backstories: Create detailed backgrounds for your characters, including their upbringing, experiences, and traumas. Understanding their pasts will inform their present actions and motivations.

Give Them Goals: Every character should have desires, whether big or small. These goals drive the plot forward and reveal important aspects of their personalities.

Create Flaws: Perfect characters are dull. Give your characters flaws and vulnerabilities to make them relatable and interesting. Flaws create opportunities for growth and conflict.

Show Their Complexity: Characters should be multi-dimensional. Explore different facets of their personalities, including their strengths, weaknesses, fears, and contradictions.

Write Distinct Dialogue: Each character should have a unique voice and speech patterns. Pay attention to vocabulary, sentence structure, and cadence to differentiate them.

Use Physical Descriptions Wisely: Describe your characters' appearances in a way that reveals something about their personalities or backgrounds. Avoid clichés and focus on meaningful details.

Reveal Through Actions: Show, don't tell, who your characters are through their actions and decisions. Actions speak louder than words and can convey subtleties that dialogue alone cannot.

Create Conflicts: Characters should face internal and external conflicts that challenge them and drive the plot forward. Conflicts reveal character and create opportunities for growth.

Write Compelling Relationships: Explore the dynamics between your characters. Develop nuanced relationships that evolve over time, reflecting the complexities of real-life connections.

Give Them Arcs: Characters should undergo growth or change throughout the story. Construct character arcs that show their transformation, whether it's overcoming obstacles, learning lessons, or making sacrifices.

Listen to Your Characters: Sometimes characters have a mind of their own. Stay open to unexpected developments and let your characters guide the story in authentic directions.

Stay True to Their Essence: While characters may evolve, they should remain true to their core identities. Ensure that their actions and decisions align with who they are at their core.

These tips focus on the art of crafting compelling characters that readers will connect with and care about, enriching your storytelling and bringing your narrative to life.

> " The worst enemy to creativity is self-doubt.

— SYLVIA PLATH

Quit doubting yourself.
You've got what it takes.

Give us a call today.

~Now accepting all genres~

1-775-996-3844

DARE TO BE A UNICORN

VICTORIA BROCK

TRIENT PRESS MAGAZINE — FEBRUARY/ MARCH

Navigating the Evolving Landscape of Modern Publishing

In the digital age, where the written word has found new avenues for expression and dissemination, the landscape of modern publishing has undergone a profound transformation. This transformation, akin to taming a literary tempest, presents both challenges and opportunities for authors, publishers, and stakeholders across the industry.

Understanding the Digital Metamorphosis

At the heart of this evolution lies the digital revolution. The advent of the internet and the ubiquity of electronic devices have democratized publishing. Anyone with a story to tell can now become an author. Traditional publishing houses, once the sole gatekeepers to literary acclaim, now coexist with self-publishing platforms, creating a diverse and dynamic marketplace.

The Digital Reader and Changing Preferences

The modern reader, armed with smartphones and e-readers, seeks instant access to a vast array of written content. This shift in consumption preferences has disrupted traditional distribution models. E-books and audiobooks, once viewed as novelties, have become mainstream, challenging the dominance of physical books.

Emerging Technologies and Innovation

Technological advancements such as artificial intelligence and blockchain are reshaping publishing in unforeseen ways. AI-driven algorithms analyze reading habits to recommend tailored content, while blockchain ensures transparency and intellectual property rights. These innovations promise efficiency and security, but also raise questions about privacy and control.

The Author's Dilemma

For authors, this new landscape presents both liberation and complexity. Self-publishing offers creative freedom, but success requires not only writing talent but also marketing savvy. Traditional publishing, on the other hand, provides access to established distribution networks, but often at the cost of creative control.

AUTHOR TIPS | TRIENT PRESS

TRIENT PRESS MAGAZINE — FEBRUARY/ MARCH

Publishing in an Age of Information

In a world inundated with information, standing out as an author or publisher is a formidable challenge. Content marketing and social media strategies have become indispensable tools for reaching and engaging with readers. Crafting a compelling online presence is as important as writing a compelling book.

The Role of Content Aggregators

Content aggregators, like Amazon and Google, have become gateways to the digital marketplace. They wield immense influence over discoverability and sales. Authors and publishers must navigate the nuances of algorithms and digital storefronts to maximize their reach.

The Ethical Implications of Digital Publishing

As publishing embraces the digital realm, ethical questions emerge. Issues of copyright infringement, data privacy, and the impact of algorithms on reading habits require thoughtful consideration. A balance must be struck between technological progress and ethical responsibility.

Balancing Tradition and Innovation

In conclusion, navigating the evolving landscape of modern publishing is a journey that requires both tradition and innovation. Authors and publishers must harness the power of technology while upholding the timeless values of storytelling and intellectual property. Success in this dynamic environment demands adaptability, creativity, and an unwavering commitment to the written word.

As we continue to traverse this literary frontier, let us remember that while the tools of publishing may change, the essence of storytelling remains constant. Whether with pen and parchment or pixels and screens, the power of words to inspire, inform, and enchant endures.

AUTHOR TIPS |TRIENT PRESS

Volition (Noah & Tessa's Story #1) A Uniform & Lace Romance
www.Goodreads.com

Tina Maurine
4.48/5.00
33 ratings 31 reviews

Freshly divorced, Navy aircraft electrician Tessa Christy is ready to embrace her newfound freedom on her six month deployment to Iceland. While working toward a coveted promotion, Tess breaks the tedium by rocking the single life: making new friends, partying, and hooking up with a hot guy or two.

The last thing Tess wants or expects is to meet someone... irresistible. Unattainable and unavailable, Noah Garren's past and present conspire to keep a promising love trapped in anger, misunderstanding–and undeniable lust.

What's a girl to do when she can't hang on... but her heart refuses to let go.

Warning: This erotic cliffhanger romance contains explicit sex scenes and is not intended for readers under the age of 18.

183 pages, Kindle Edition

First published June 5, 2018

MAXIMIZING YOUR DIGITAL FOOTPRINT:
STRATEGIES FOR AUTHORS IN THE SOCIAL MEDIA AGE

In today's interconnected world, authors find themselves not only as wordsmiths but also as digital trailblazers. The digital age has ushered in new opportunities and challenges, demanding that authors master the art of maximizing their digital footprint to thrive in the social media age.

The Digital Age of Authorship

Gone are the days when an author's responsibility ended with the final sentence of a manuscript. In the digital era, the journey is just beginning. Authors are now expected to be active participants in the promotion and distribution of their work. This paradigm shift requires a strategic approach to managing one's digital presence.

Building Your Author Brand

The foundation of a strong digital footprint is a well-crafted author brand. Your brand is not just about your books; it's about you as a writer and a personality. Define your unique voice and message. Are you the suspense thriller maestro, the romantic wordsmith, or the non-fiction authority? Your brand should reflect your writing style and values.

Choosing the Right Social Media Platforms

Not all social media platforms are created equal, and nor are they equally effective for all authors. Consider your target audience and genre. For visual genres like fashion or cookbooks, platforms like Instagram or Pinterest may excel. Thought-provoking authors might find Twitter to be their domain. The key is to align your platform choice with your brand and audience.

Content Is King: Quality over Quantity

In the race to make an impact, it's easy to fall into the trap of posting frequently without considering the quality of your content. Engage your audience with meaningful posts. Share insights into your writing process, behind-the-scenes glimpses, and thought-provoking questions. Quality content resonates, fosters engagement, and builds a loyal readership.

Consistency and Authenticity

Consistency is the cornerstone of a powerful digital presence. Maintain a regular posting schedule, but do so authentically. Authenticity builds trust with your audience. Share personal anecdotes, triumphs, and challenges. Show the human side of the author behind the words.

Engagement and Interaction

Social media is a two-way street. Engage with your readers, respond to comments, and initiate conversations. Hosting Q&A sessions or virtual book clubs can forge strong connections. Remember, social media is not just a broadcasting tool; it's a platform for genuine interaction.

TRIENT PRESS MAGAZINE   FEBRUARY/ MARCH

Harnessing Analytics and Data

Don't rely on guesswork. Social media platforms provide robust analytics. Monitor your performance, track which posts resonate, and adjust your strategy accordingly. Data-driven decisions can significantly enhance your digital footprint.

Collaborations and Influencer Marketing

Consider collaborations with fellow authors or influencers in your niche. Cross-promotion can expand your reach exponentially. Partnering with influencers who align with your brand can introduce your work to a broader, engaged audience.

Ethical Considerations

In this digital age, ethical considerations are paramount. Respect your readers' privacy, obtain proper permissions for content use, and adhere to platform guidelines. Ethical behavior not only safeguards your reputation but also fosters trust.

Adapting to the Ever-Changing Landscape

The digital landscape is in perpetual motion. Stay abreast of emerging trends and technologies. What worked yesterday may not work tomorrow. Adaptability is the key to long-term success.

In conclusion, authors in the social media age must be digital strategists as much as they are wordsmiths. Maximizing your digital footprint is not a one-time endeavor but an ongoing journey of self-discovery and engagement. It's about crafting a compelling author brand, sharing meaningful content, building authentic relationships, and staying agile in an ever-evolving digital world. Embrace the power of your digital footprint, and let it amplify your literary voice.

AUTHOR TIPS |TRIENT PRESS

Collaborative Writing in the Digital Era: Unleash Your Creative Synergy

In an age where information travels at the speed of thought and creativity knows no bounds, collaborative writing has evolved into an exhilarating journey that transcends the limitations of solitary authorship. Join us as we embark on a riveting exploration of the digital tools and techniques that can transform your collaborative writing endeavors into works of literary brilliance.

The Digital Revolution and Collaborative Magic

The digital era has unlocked new dimensions of creative synergy. Collaborative writing, once constrained by geographical barriers, now flourishes in a global playground. Authors from diverse corners of the world converge to craft narratives that blend their unique voices, resulting in literary alchemy.

Diving into the Collaborative Toolbox

To succeed in this collaborative renaissance, authors must wield a formidable toolbox of digital instruments:

Cloud-Based Writing Platforms

Google Docs, Microsoft 365, and other cloud-based tools empower authors to co-create seamlessly. Real-time editing, comments, and version history erase the confines of physical distance, fostering synchronicity in the creative process.

Virtual Brainstorming Sessions

Zoom, Slack, and virtual meetings recreate the magic of in-person brainstorming. Exchange ideas, shape plot twists, and fuel each other's imaginations through dynamic discussions.

Social Media Communities

Dive into writing communities on platforms like Reddit and Twitter. Share snippets, seek feedback, and connect with kindred spirits who share your literary zeal.

Collaborative Editing Tools

Tools like Grammarly and ProWritingAid ensure uniformity in style and grammar, ensuring a polished manuscript that seamlessly combines the voices of multiple authors.

TECHNIQUES FOR HARMONIOUS COLLABORATION

Unlocking the full potential of collaborative writing requires finesse and artistry:

DEFINE ROLES AND GOALS: CLEARLY DELINEATE EACH AUTHOR'S ROLE AND CONTRIBUTION. ESTABLISH COMMON OBJECTIVES TO GUIDE THE CREATIVE PROCESS.

EMBRACE DIVERSE PERSPECTIVES: COLLABORATIVE WRITING THRIVES ON DIVERSITY. EMBRACE VARYING VIEWPOINTS, BACKGROUNDS, AND WRITING STYLES TO ENRICH THE NARRATIVE TAPESTRY.

MAINTAIN EFFECTIVE COMMUNICATION: OPEN AND REGULAR COMMUNICATION IS THE LIFEBLOOD OF COLLABORATION. SHARE PROGRESS UPDATES, ADDRESS CONCERNS PROMPTLY, AND CELEBRATE MILESTONES.

SET DEADLINES AND MILESTONES: A STRUCTURED TIMELINE ENSURES PROGRESS. SET ACHIEVABLE MILESTONES TO KEEP THE CREATIVE ENERGY FLOWING.

RESPECT CREATIVE AUTONOMY: WHILE COLLABORATION IS KEY, RESPECT EACH AUTHOR'S CREATIVE AUTONOMY. ALLOW ROOM FOR INDIVIDUAL EXPRESSION WITHIN THE COLLECTIVE WORK.

TRIENT PRESS MAGAZINE   FEBRUARY/ MARCH

The Thrill of Collaborative Triumph

In the digital era, collaborative writing is an electrifying adventure, where each keystroke echoes with collective imagination. Authors engage in a symphony of creativity, where the sum is undeniably greater than its parts.

Together, they breathe life into characters, craft intricate plots, and birth worlds anew. Collaborative writing is not just about shared words; it's about shared dreams, aspirations, and the exhilarating realization that creativity knows no boundaries.

LASTLY, Your Collaborative Odyssey Awaits

As we sail through the digital seas of collaborative writing, remember that the journey is as important as the destination. Embrace the tools and techniques, respect the diverse voices, and revel in the thrilling tapestry of creativity that unfolds before you. Collaborative writing in the digital era is not just a literary endeavor; it's a transformative experience where the collective imagination ignites into a blaze of literary brilliance.

Are you ready to embark on your collaborative odyssey? The digital era beckons, and the world awaits your literary masterpiece.

AUTHOR TIPS |TRIENT PRESS

Trient Press

Trient Press Publishing

e at Trient Press, our obvious l is to put our authors' books n front of as many eyes as sible; to that end though, we o not value a book solely in es. A book that sells a million opies is no more important han a title that sells only a undred. Many books have a reater value in the message in the pages, than the bills it outs in our author's wallet. gned with this mindset, the thors we currently have often participate in charity hologies, which all proceeds o to a selected non-profit or charity group.

Trient Basmak

Trient Besmak is set to be our International leg. Set In Instanbul, Turkey, we high expectations from this office. Adding translations from English to Turkish and vice versa. In addition to signing authors from the region.

We will be working with area prepsientives to distribute our current collection in the country while bringing the voices of the our new authors to our current markets.

Trient Press Printing & Distribution

Trient Printing and Distribution (TP&D) will focus on the printing of books, magazines and other media on-site, leading the way using mostly green-energy in its printing, cutting, and binding, while also keeping the carbon footprint below industry standards without cutting corners on quality or production speeds. Following the printing and binding, printed materials will then be entered directly into the distribution channel to be delivered to the ultimate reader or user.

Trient Evolve

Trient Evolve is set to be our marketing agency which will continue to partner with our small business outreach. Continuing our work with Dove & Dragon Radio and Trientrepreneur Magazine. Dedicated to the sole purpose of helping small business and author in reaching their audience.

ESCAPE *the ordinary*

SUBMISSIONS@TRIENTPRESS.COM

Trient Press

Mission Statement

Since its conception, Trient Press has always been about more than just meeting author expectations, we've always aimed to exceed them.

Trient Press has a simple mission statement:

Trient Press is a publishing company focused on producing high-quality, ORIGINAL e-books, paperbacks, and hardcovers, which exceed our author clients' needs and goals.

We support creative, non-hateful expression across multiple fictional genres.
We care about your publishing success and will work tirelessly to meet your goals and get your book in the hands of readers everywhere.

1-775-996-3844

TRIENT PRESS MAGAZINE FEBRUARY/ MARCH

FROM DRAFT TO BESTSELLER:
Navigating the 2024 Publishing Process

In the literary world of 2024, where the boundaries of creativity and technology continue to expand, the path from draft to bestseller is an exhilarating voyage filled with new challenges and opportunities. Join us as we embark on this thrilling journey through the modern publishing process, where success awaits those who navigate the current of innovation and adaptability.

THE EVOLUTION OF PUBLISHING

The publishing landscape has morphed into a dynamic realm reflecting the digital age's impact on literature. Today, authors and publishers alike must navigate multifaceted terrain where traditional and digital publishing coexist, giving rise to fresh possibilities.

CRAFTING YOUR MANUSCRIPT

At the heart of every bestseller lies a meticulously crafted manuscript. Authors continue to hone their storytelling skills, but now they must also consider the digital format. Writing for an audience that toggles between e-readers, audiobooks, and print requires versatility and adaptability.

AUTHOR TIPS |TRIENT PRESS

TRIENT PRESS MAGAZINE   FEBRUARY/ MARCH

THE AGENT'S ROLE IN 2024

In this era, literary agents are not mere gatekeepers; they are shrewd navigators of the digital domain. They harness data analytics to pinpoint market trends, guiding authors toward genres and themes that resonate with today's readers.

THE DIGITAL PUBLISHING REVOLUTION

Digital publishing platforms have democratized the industry, allowing authors to bypass traditional gatekeepers. Self-publishing has evolved from a niche endeavor to a powerful option for authors who wish to retain creative control and a larger share of royalties.

ENGAGING READERS IN A DIGITAL WORLD

In the age of information overload, standing out is a formidable challenge. Authors must embrace content marketing, social media engagement, and innovative promotional strategies to connect with their readers. Building a dedicated online following is a crucial step toward bestseller status.

EMERGING TECHNOLOGIES AND AUGMENTED REALITY

2024 heralds the advent of augmented reality (AR) literature, where immersive storytelling experiences blend the digital and physical worlds. Authors can experiment with AR to engage readers on a deeper level, creating interactive narratives that captivate the imagination.

PUBLISHING ETHICS AND DIGITAL RIGHTS

The digital landscape brings ethical concerns to the forefront. Authors and publishers must navigate issues of copyright, privacy, and data security, ensuring that readers' trust remains intact.

AUTHOR TIPS |TRIENT PRESS

GLOBAL REACH AND TRANSLATION

The global reach of digital publishing means authors can connect with readers worldwide. Translation services and international marketing strategies open doors to new audiences, expanding the potential for bestseller status.

THE POWER OF DATA AND ANALYTICS

Data-driven decision-making has become paramount. Authors an publishers rely on analytics to tailor their marketing efforts, optimize pricing, and refine content strategies, increasing the chances of reaching bestseller lists.

ADAPTING TO THE UNPREDICTABLE

The publishing landscape is in constant flux. Flexibility, adaptability, and an unwavering commitment to the craft are essential. As trends shift and technologies evolve, the most successful authors and publishers are those who embrace change.

IN CONCLUSION: CHARTING YOUR BESTSELLER JOURNEY

In 2024, the publishing process is a multifaceted expedition filled with innovation and opportunity. Authors and publishers who leverage the digital landscape, harness the power of data, and embrace the evolving nature of the industry are poised to navigate the course from draft to bestseller.

The literary world of 2024 beckons with limitless potential. It's a world where the creative spirit finds new wings, and the journey from draft to bestseller is an adventure worth embarking upon. Are you ready to chart your bestseller journey in this exciting era of publishing?

At Trient Evolve, we are committed to empowering entrepreneurs and business owners with cutting-edge solutions to drive growth, efficiency, and success in today's dynamic marketplace. Explore our comprehensive range of business solutions, carefully curated to address the unique challenges and opportunities your business may encounter.

TRIENT
EVOLVE

BALANCING CREATIVITY AND COMMERCE:

Pricing Strategies for Independent Authors

In the enchanting realm of literature, where words become worlds and stories are spun from the threads of imagination, independent authors wield a unique power. They are not just creators of narratives; they are entrepreneurs of creativity, sculptors of dreams, and architects of literary journeys. Yet, amidst the boundless tapestry of creativity, there exists a pragmatic thread that weaves through the fabric of their craft – pricing.

For independent authors, the art of pricing is a delicate dance, a symphony that harmonizes the realms of creativity and commerce. It's the skillful navigation of a labyrinth where every choice echoes through the corridors of their literary aspirations and economic realities. How do they assign value to their labor of love? How do they ensure their works reach the hands of eager readers while sustaining their creative pursuits?

In this article, we embark on a journey into the world of pricing strategies for independent authors. We delve deep into the principles, considerations, and intricacies that underpin the art of setting a price tag on creativity. It's a journey where we illuminate the path to finding that delicate equilibrium, where the value of an author's work meets the expectations of their audience.

As we navigate this terrain, we'll explore the fundamentals of pricing, the factors that influence it, and the strategies that transform a manuscript into a marketable masterpiece. We'll unveil the secrets of pricing that empower independent authors to sustain their artistic vision and cultivate a loyal readership.

In the enchanting realm of literature, where words become worlds and stories are spun from the threads of imagination, independent authors wield a unique power. They are not just creators of narratives; they are entrepreneurs of creativity, sculptors of dreams, and architects of literary journeys. Yet, amidst the boundless tapestry of creativity, there exists a pragmatic thread that weaves through the fabric of their craft – pricing.

For independent authors, the art of pricing is a delicate dance, a symphony that harmonizes the realms of creativity and commerce. It's the skillful navigation of a labyrinth where every choice echoes through the corridors of their literary aspirations and economic realities. How do they assign value to their labor of love? How do they ensure their works reach the hands of eager readers while sustaining their creative pursuits?

In this article, we embark on a journey into the world of pricing strategies for independent authors. We delve deep into the principles, considerations, and intricacies that underpin the art of setting a price tag on creativity. It's a journey where we illuminate the path to finding that delicate equilibrium, where the value of an author's work meets the expectations of their audience.

As we navigate this terrain, we'll explore the fundamentals of pricing, the factors that influence it, and the strategies that transform a manuscript into a marketable masterpiece. We'll unveil the secrets of pricing that empower independent authors to sustain their artistic vision and cultivate a loyal readership.

But before we embark on this enlightening journey, let us pause and reflect on the profound intersection of creativity and commerce that defines the world of independent authorship. It's a place where the passion for storytelling mingles with the practicality of running a literary business, and where the dreams of authors take flight through the pages of their books.

Join us as we uncover the strategies and insights that will help independent authors strike that elusive balance – where creativity thrives, and commerce sustains. Welcome to the world where artistry meets economics, where words have value, and where the journey from manuscript to bestseller begins with a well-crafted pricing strategy.

In the intricate symphony of independent authorship, where creativity meets commerce, pricing strategies are the notes that harmonize the composition. As you venture forth in your literary journey, remember that the choices you make in pricing are not just about numbers but about the value you place on your craft.

In the realm of independent authorship, where you are not only the writer but also the entrepreneur, the conductor, and the impresario, finding that perfect balance between creativity and commerce is both the challenge and the reward. It's about ensuring that your creative labor is justly compensated while remaining accessible to your cherished readers.

As you navigate the path ahead, consider the insights we've explored in this article – from understanding your costs and market dynamics to evaluating the unique value of your work. These are the guiding principles that will lead you toward a pricing strategy that resonates with both your artistic aspirations and your commercial goals.

Remember, your work is a labor of love, a testament to your dedication and imagination. It deserves to shine not only in the world of creativity but also in the realm of commerce. Pricing it thoughtfully is your way of ensuring that your voice is heard, your stories are shared, and your journey as an independent author is both fulfilling and sustainable.

In the evolving landscape of independent authorship, the pricing strategies you employ become more than just numbers; they become the bridge that connects your creativity with the world. They are the means by which your stories transcend the confines of your imagination to touch the hearts and minds of readers near and far.

So, dear independent author, as you set your pricing strategies in motion, do so with the knowledge that you are not merely pricing a book; you are valuing a work of art, a piece of your soul, and a connection with your audience. Balancing creativity and commerce is not compromise; it's a beautiful synthesis of passion and pragmatism that allows you to share your stories with the world while ensuring your journey as an independent author thrives.

May your words continue to inspire, your stories continue to captivate, and your pricing strategies continue to strike the harmonious chord that resonates with both your readers and your artistic spirit.

Farewell on your continuing journey of creativity, commerce and literary excellence.

DIVINE CONNECTIONS

www.divineconnectionsmagazine.com/

The Art of Self-Promotion: Building Your Brand as an Author

In the hallowed halls of literature, where stories take flight and words paint vivid landscapes of the imagination, authors embark on a quest that stretches far beyond the pages of their manuscripts. It's a journey of literary exploration, of creative revelation, and, in the digital age, an artful expedition into the world of self-promotion.

As an author, your ability to craft compelling narratives is the heart of your craft, but it is only the beginning. To flourish in the literary landscape of today, where every voice seeks to be heard in the cacophony of information, you must become the maestro of self-promotion. You are not just an author; you are the torchbearer of your literary brand.

In this article, we delve into the art of self-promotion – the strategic masterpiece that allows you to shine amidst the literary constellations. It's a journey where creativity extends beyond the pages of your book, into the realm of marketing, engagement, and brand building. It's about transforming your literary identity into a beacon that guides readers through the vast cosmos of books and stories.

TRIENT PRESS MAGAZINE   FEBRUARY/MARCH

PIn the hallowed halls of literature, where stories take flight and words paint vivid landscapes of the imagination, authors embark on a quest that stretches far beyond the pages of their manuscripts. It's a journey of literary exploration, of creative revelation, and, in the digital age, an artful expedition into the world of self-promotion.

As an author, your ability to craft compelling narratives is the heart of your craft, but it is only the beginning. To flourish in the literary landscape of today, where every voice seeks to be heard in the cacophony of information, you must become the maestro of self-promotion. You are not just an author; you are the torchbearer of your literary brand.

In this article, we delve into the art of self-promotion – the strategic masterpiece that allows you to shine amidst the literary constellations. It's a journey where creativity extends beyond the pages of your book, into the realm of marketing, engagement, and brand building. It's about transforming your literary identity into a beacon that guides readers through the vast cosmos of books and stories.

But self-promotion is not about brash advertising or self-aggrandizement; it's about crafting a compelling narrative that extends beyond your manuscript. It's about telling the story of your authorship, your journey, and the worlds you create. It's about connecting with readers on a deeper level, fostering a loyal following, and turning the spotlight onto your literary brilliance.

As we embark on this journey together, we'll unravel the strategies, principles, and techniques that empower you to build your author brand. We'll explore the nuances of storytelling in marketing, the secrets of engaging with your audience, and the transformative power of self-promotion that elevates your craft from mere words on a page to a captivating literary odyssey.

But before we delve into the artistry of self-promotion, let us pause to appreciate the literary odyssey that lies before us. It's a journey where the stories you tell extend beyond the confines of your books, and where your author brand becomes a constellation in the vast universe of literature.

TRIENT PRESS MAGAZINE					FEBRUARY/ MARCH

THE TRANSFORMATIVE POWER OF BRANDING

Your author brand is not just a logo or a tagline; it's the essence of your literary identity. Consistency in branding, from your book covers to your online presence, creates a memorable image. A well-crafted author brand not only attracts readers but also communicates professionalism and trustworthiness.

So, dear author, as we embark on this literary voyage together, prepare to unleash the art of self-promotion, to illuminate your author brand, and to set sail on a literary odyssey that will captivate minds, touch hearts, and leave a luminous trail in the literary cosmos. Welcome to the art of self-promotion, where your journey as an author reaches new heights of creativity and engagement.

CRAFTING YOUR LITERARY NARRATIVE

At the heart of self-promotion lies the art of crafting your literary narrative. It's not just about selling books; it's about telling your story as an author. What inspired your literary journey? What themes and worlds do you explore? Who are the characters that inhabit your imagination? Your narrative is the thread that connects you with your readers, weaving a tapestry of connection and understanding.

ENGAGEMENT: THE HEARTBEAT OF YOUR BRAND

In the digital age, engagement is the heartbeat of your author brand. Social media, author websites, and virtual events offer platforms to engage with your audience. Interact with readers, share insights into your writing process, and invite them into your literary world. It's the authenticity of these interactions that forges lasting connections.

BUILDING A LOYAL FOLLOWING

Self-promotion is not a one-time endeavor; it's a continuous journey of building a loyal following. Cultivate a community of readers who resonate with your work. Offer them exclusive content, behind-the-scenes glimpses, and a sense of belonging to something extraordinary – your literary universe.

TURNING YOUR PASSION INTO VISIBILITY

Passion fuels self-promotion. Let your enthusiasm for your craft shine through in every engagement. Whether it's writing blog posts, participating in book signings, or creating captivating social media content, infuse your passion into every endeavor. It's this fervor that captivates and inspires others.

As we conclude our exploration of the art of self-promotion for authors, remember that this journey is about self-aggrandizement but about elevating your craft and connecting with those who share your passion for storytelling. It's about being the torchbearer of your literary vision and guiding readers through the magical realms you create.

Your literary odyssey, dear author, is an ongoing adventure where each word you write and each interaction you have builds a constellation in the literary universe. Self-promotion is the compass that guides you, the bridge that connects you with readers, and the anthem that celebrates your creativity.

As you continue your journey, may you find joy in every chapter, strength in every word, and inspiration in every connection you make. Your story as an author is a tapestry woven with the threads of self-promotion, and it's a tale that will resonate with readers for generations to come.

Embrace the art of self-promotion, illuminate your author brand, and embark on a literary odyssey that transcends the boundaries of imagination. Your journey as an author is a beacon in the world of literature, lighting the way for those who seek the magic of storytelling.

Welcome to the art of self-promotion, where your literary odyssey unfolds with brilliance and grace.

THE MYSTERIOUS INTERSECTION OF DREAMS AND DEATH:
A Conversation with Bryon Ehlmann

BY M.L. RUSCSAK

In an enlightening and somewhat unconventional encounter, I sat down with Bryon Ehlmann, a retired computer science professor turned author, who delves deep into the enigmatic realms of consciousness, dreams, and the afterlife. Ehlmann's journey from the logic-driven world of computer science to exploring the profound questions of existence is as fascinating as it is unexpected.

Ehlmann, with the relaxed demeanor of someone who's spent years in academia, explains his shift from computer science to his current passion. "I retired early from computer science because I got kind of tired of all the technical stuff and having to keep up with things," he shares. This transition marked the beginning of his quest into the bigger questions of life, a journey that led him down an extraordinary path of self-discovery and intellectual exploration.

It was a dream, quite literally, that sparked Ehlmann's profound interest in the afterlife and consciousness. He recalls a moment of epiphany upon waking from a particularly vivid dream. "For the first time in my life, I asked myself the question, what would happen if I hadn't woken up? How would I ever know the dream was over?" This curiosity about the unobservable moment of transition from life to death led him to develop his theory, detailed in his book, "A Natural Afterlife Discovered, The Newfound Psychological Reality That Awaits Us at Death."

Ehlmann's theory is a thought-provoking blend of cognitive science, philosophy, and personal introspection. He suggests that in the absence of a supernatural afterlife, our last moment of consciousness may stretch indefinitely. "You are never going to lose your sense of self at death," he posits. This idea challenges conventional notions of mortality and the afterlife, proposing a unique perspective on what awaits us beyond.

Throughout our conversation, Ehlmann's academic background is evident in his analytical approach to such a mystical topic. He likens the human experience of consciousness to the frames in a film, discrete moments that collectively form our perception of reality. His theory is not just an intellectual exercise; it carries profound implications about how we perceive life and death.

As Ehlmann elaborates on his theory, he maintains a balance between the scientific and the speculative, always grounding his hypotheses in observable phenomena like dreams and near-death experiences. He is quick to differentiate his ideas from other theories that venture into the realms of dreams as alternate realities or simulations.

Ehlmann's journey from the structured world of computer science to exploring the intangible aspects of human consciousness is a testament to the unending quest for knowledge and understanding that defines us as humans. His insights offer a fresh perspective on the age-old questions of existence, encouraging us to ponder the nature of our consciousness and the mysteries that lie beyond the veil of death.

In a world where the boundaries between science and philosophy increasingly blur, Bryon Ehlmann stands as a fascinating figure, bridging these realms with his unique insights. His exploration into the unknown is a reminder that sometimes, the most profound discoveries come from the simplest questions.

AUTHOR SPOTLIGHT | TRIENT PRESS

JORDAN BROODY
ARCHONIS

FROM CLASSICAL SCORES TO COSMIC WARS:

The Creative Odyssey of Jordan Broody and M.L. Ruscscak

In an engaging encounter, I had the pleasure of speaking with Jordan, an author whose journey from classical music composer to science fiction writer captures the essence of creative evolution. His debut novel, 'Archonis,' is not just a book; it's an immersive experience where music and storytelling intertwine to create something truly unique.

Jordan's transition from composing epic scores to penning an epic tale is a story in itself. "I always wrote different scores...like epic scores from movies," he explains. The idea to blend this musical talent with narrative storytelling was a stroke of creative genius. "What would be a really cool idea would be to make a story and then align the music with it," he thought. And thus, 'Archonis' was born.

The book revolves around Darius Jatora, a character Jordan describes as a "space samurai," a hunter undertaking missions across the galaxy. The plot thickens as Darius uncovers an ancient prophecy, setting him on a collision course with destiny and moral dilemma. Jordan's description of his protagonis is vivid and engaging, evoking images of a galaxy-spanning adventure.

But 'Archonis' is more than just a space odyssey. It's a tale of conflict and prophecy, where the hero must choose between his sacred profession and the fate of the galaxy. This conflict is mirrored in the story's antagonist, Zin-Zorath, who, while opposing Darius, shares a similar goal: to save the galaxy.

Jordan's ambition doesn't stop with 'Archonis'. He reveals that it's the first in a trilogy, with all three parts already written, the first already gracing the shelves. Self-publishing on Amazon and aiming for larger publishing houses, Jordan's journey mirrors the challenges and triumphs of many independent authors.

But writing is just one facet of Jordan's life. He juggles his passion for storytelling with a career in medical sales and his responsibilities as a father. "It's difficult to do everything at once being a part-time writer, but if it's something that you love, then you just find a way to get it in there," he shares, a sentiment that resonates with many striving to balance their passions with their professions.

Looking ahead, Jordan has his sights set on a dark fantasy series, hinting at a shift from cosmic battles to a more sinister, earthly realm. His creative process is ongoing, a perpetual journey of exploration and expression.

For those eager to dive into the world of 'Archonis' or learn more about Jordan's multifaceted life, he invites readers and listeners to his website and Instagram. His story is a testament to the power of passion and the endless possibilities that arise when one dares to dream and create.

Jordan's journey from the rhythmic cadences of classical music to the expansive narratives of science fiction is a reminder that creativity knows no bounds. In 'Archonis,' we find not just a story, but a symphony of ideas, a harmonious blend of art forms that speaks to the heart of innovation and imagination.

ROOSEVELT WILLIAMS III: A BEACON OF COMMUNITY EMPOWERMENT AND PEACE IN SAN DIEGO

by: M.L.Ruscsak

In the vibrant tapestry of San Diego's community leaders, Roosevelt Williams III stands out as a luminary figure, whose profound contributions to local economic development and peace initiatives have not only garnered widespread attention but also sparked a transformative movement. As the CEO of Young Black & N' Business (YB&NB), Williams has become synonymous with the ethos of empowerment, championing the cause of the underserved and injecting a renewed sense of hope and opportunity into the heart of the community.

His journey, marked by a deep commitment to service and an unwavering dedication to the greater good, resonates throughout San Diego. At the helm of YB&NB, Williams has meticulously crafted a platform that transcends mere business development; it is a beacon for those seeking guidance, support, and inspiration. His efforts extend beyond the confines of conventional leadership, embodying a holistic approach that intertwines economic advancement with social upliftment.

Williams's philosophy, rooted in the wisdom passed down by his great-grandfather, Matthew Cook Sr., emphasizes integrity, diligence, and community welfare. This mantra, "IF IT IS TO BE, IT IS UP TO US," serves as a guiding principle for his leadership, encapsulating his belief in the power of collective action and shared responsibility.

His journey, marked by a deep commitment to service and an unwavering dedication to the greater good, resonates throughout San Diego. At the helm of YB&NB, Williams has meticulously crafted a platform that transcends mere business development; it is a beacon for those seeking guidance, support, and inspiration. His efforts extend beyond the confines of conventional leadership, embodying a holistic approach that intertwines economic advancement with social upliftment.

Williams's philosophy, rooted in the wisdom passed down by his great-grandfather, Matthew Cook Sr., emphasizes integrity, diligence, and community welfare. This mantra, "IF IT IS TO BE, IT IS UP TO US," serves as a guiding principle for his leadership, encapsulating his belief in the power of collective action and shared responsibility.

The impact of Williams's work reverberates far beyond the borders of San Diego. His efforts in conflict resolution and peacebuilding serve as a model for communities worldwide, demonstrating the transformative power of dialogue and understanding. In a world often riven by differences, Williams's ability to bridge gaps and foster a spirit of togetherness stands as a beacon of hope and a testament to the enduring strength of human connection.

Williams's leadership is not confined to the boardroom or the conference hall; it extends to the streets and neighborhoods where real change is felt. As a Community Development Specialist for the City of San Diego, he has spearheaded critical projects aimed at revitalizing under-resourced areas, bringing economic opportunities to those who need them most. His role in initiatives like the Promise Zones Initiative showcases his dedication to effecting tangible, positive change, laying the groundwork for long-term prosperity and peace.

Through YB&NB, Williams empowers aspiring entrepreneurs with practical workshops, mentorship programs, and educational initiatives, fostering not only individual success but also community resilience and progress. His commitment to charitable endeavors further amplifies his impact, ensuring that the growth and success facilitated by YB&NB are shared with those in need.

Signature events like the Black & Gold Gala serve as vibrant celebrations of the community's achievements and aspirations, reflecting Williams's dedication to unity and progress. These gatherings not only honor individual successes but also reaffirm the collective commitment to building a brighter future together.

In essence, Roosevelt Williams III embodies the essence of transformative leadership, igniting change and fostering unity through his unwavering dedication to community empowerment. His story serves as a testament to the enduring power of service and collaboration, inspiring others to join in the journey towards a more inclusive and prosperous society. As Williams continues to shape the landscape of community development in San Diego and beyond, his legacy serves as a beacon of hope and a model for future generations.

AMPLIFY YOUR INFLUENCE AND EMPOWER YOUR JOURNEY
WITH ATS LEADS

WELCOME TO ATS LEADS – YOUR POWERHOUSE FOR ELEVATING YOUR IMPACT IN THE WORLD.

Your Ultimate Lead Generation Solution! Get At Least 10,000 High-Quality and Tailored Leads a Month

MAXIMIZE YOUR SOCIAL MEDIA REACH:
DOMINATE GOOGLE WITH TARGETED HASHTAGS AND KEYWORDS:

SEIZE THE MOMENT TO EXPAND YOUR INFLUENCE AND EMPOWER LIVES

magine harnessing the vast resources of Google's expansive public database, the precision of social media platforms, the reach of targeted hashtags, and the specificity of email lists to connect with individuals eager to embark on transformative journeys with you. Discover a treasure trove of clients and mentees who are not just seeking guidance but are ready to embrace profound change. Seize the moment, share your wisdom, and watch your influence expand! 🌟📸

Join the ranks of mentors, life coaches, and spiritual leaders who have already harnessed the transformative power of ATS Leads.

Unlock your capacity to empower lives with ATS Leads. Seize the moment and witness your influence soar.

Are you prepared to amplify your impact and inspire meaningful change? Experience the dynamic capabilities of ATS Leads today!

PHONE: (409)-457-6304

WEB: https://atsleads.net/

GLOBAL ECONOMIC TRENDS: CHALLENGES AND OPPORTUNITIES IN 2024

In the ever-evolving landscape of global economics, the year 2024 brings forth a tapestry of challenges and opportunities. As nations grapple with the aftermath of unprecedented events and adapt to the forces of technology and innovation, the global economic stage is set for a transformative journey.

In this article, we delve into the key trends, challenges, and opportunities that define the global economic outlook for 2024.

DIGITAL TRANSFORMATION AND AUTOMATION

The acceleration of digital transformation is a defining trend. Industries are embracing automation, artificial intelligence, and data analytics to enhance efficiency and competitiveness. While this offers opportunities for growth, it also poses challenges in terms of workforce adaptation and cybersecurity.

THE AFTERMATH OF THE PANDEMIC

The COVID-19 pandemic, which disrupted economies worldwide, continues to cast its shadow in 2024. Nations face the challenge of reviving their economies while navigating public health concerns. Recovery strategies must balance economic growth with the imperative of safeguarding public health.

RESHAPING OF SUPPLY CHAINS

The pandemic exposed vulnerabilities in global supply chains. In response, nations are reevaluating and diversifying their supply chain networks. Opportunities emerge for countries to strengthen domestic production and reduce reliance on single-source suppliers.

ECONOMICS |TRIENT PRESS

Impact from Transformative, Global Changes

THE RISE OF SUSTAINABLE INVESTING

Sustainability takes center stage as investors increasingly prioritize Environmental, Social, and Governance (ESG) factors. Companies that align with ESG principles are better positioned to attract investment. Nations are also integrating sustainability goals into economic policies.

THE GEOPOLITICAL LANDSCAPE

Geopolitical tensions and trade disputes remain a key challenge. As nations assert their economic interests, collaboration becomes crucial. Diplomacy and international cooperation are vital in navigating these complex dynamics.

THE GIG ECONOMY AND WORKFORCE SHIFTS

The gig economy continues to expand, transforming traditional employment structures. While it offers flexibility, it also raises concerns about worker rights and social safety nets. Policymakers must adapt labor regulations to address these shifts.

ENERGY TRANSITION AND CLIMATE GOALS

Energy transition toward renewable sources gains momentum. Nations are setting ambitious climate goals, offering opportunities in clean energy industries. Simultaneously, this transition poses challenges for fossil fuel-dependent economies.

THE DIGITAL CURRENCY FRONTIER

Central bank digital currencies (CBDCs) are on the rise, with some nations exploring their potential launch. This could reshape the global financial system, enhancing cross-border transactions and financial inclusion while posing regulatory challenges.

THE ROLE OF ECONOMIC RESILIENCE

Building economic resilience is paramount. Nations are diversifying revenue sources, bolstering healthcare infrastructure, and investing in education and innovation to mitigate future shocks.

As we navigate the global economic landscape in 2024, it becomes evident that challenges and opportunities are two sides of the same coin. The pandemic accelerated changes that were already underway, ushering in a new era of digitalization, sustainability, and adaptability.

For nations and businesses alike, success lies in their ability to embrace these trends, adapt swiftly, and forge collaborative solutions to global challenges. The world of economics is evolving, and the year 2024 marks a significant waypoint in this transformative journey.

It is through strategic planning, innovation, and international cooperation that nations and businesses will unlock the full potential of the global economic landscape in 2024 and beyond. As we confront challenges and seize opportunities, the resilience and ingenuity of economies worldwide continue to shape the path forward in this dynamic era of global economics.

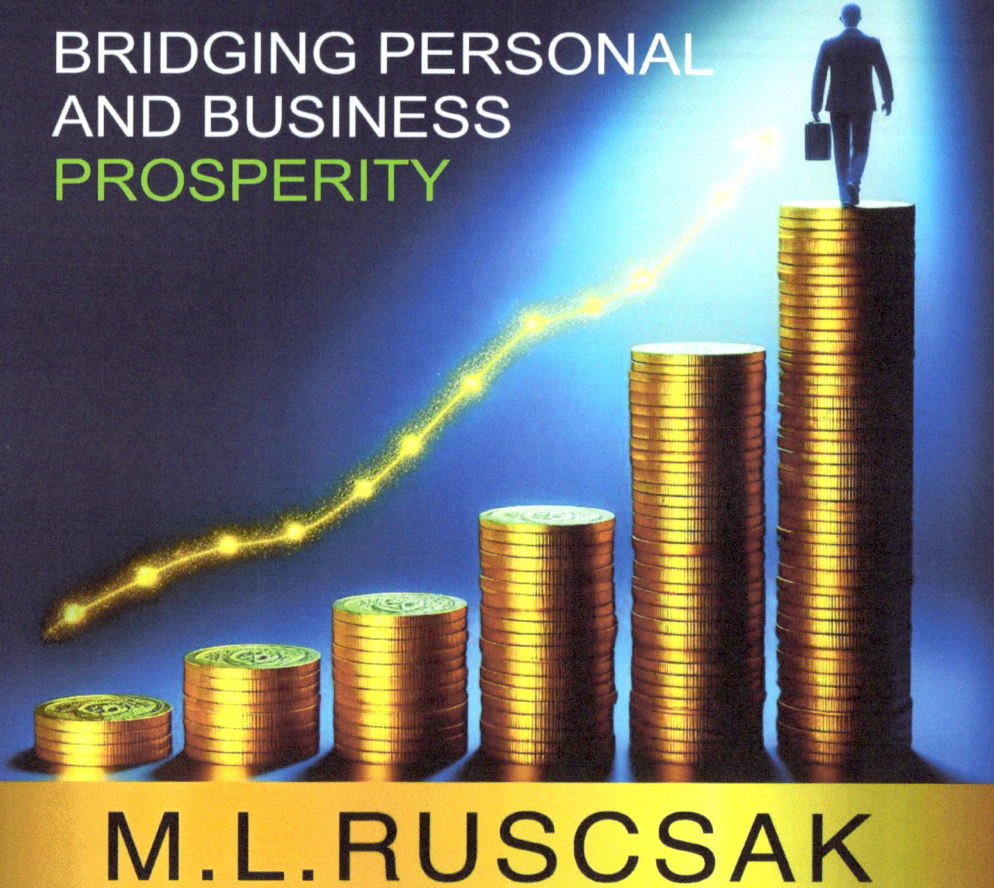

TRIENT PRESS MAGAZINE   FEBRUARY/ MARCH

NAVIGATING ECONOMIC UNCERTAINTY: INVESTMENT STRATEGIES FOR TURBULENT TIMES

In the complex and ever-shifting landscape of global economics, uncertainty has become a constant companion. The financial world is no stranger to turbulence, and investors find themselves traversing a terrain marked by unpredictability. In these challenging times, the adage "knowledge is power" holds truer than ever, as informed investment strategies become paramount for safeguarding wealth and capitalizing on opportunities.

Understanding the Current Landscape

The first step in navigating economic uncertainty is to understand the forces at play. In 2024, the world finds itself at the crossroads of recovery from the COVID-19 pandemic, geopolitical tensions, technological disruption, and shifting market dynamics. Each of these factors contributes to the complex tapestry of global economics.

The Role of Diversification

Diversification remains a stalwart strategy in the face of uncertainty. A well-structured investment portfolio should encompass a mix of asset classes, including stocks, bonds, real estate, and alternative investments. Diversification spreads risk and reduces exposure to the vagaries of any single market.

The Importance of Risk Assessment

Risk assessment is the bedrock of informed investing. Investors should conduct a comprehensive evaluation of their risk tolerance, financial goals, and investment horizon. With a clear understanding of these factors, they can tailor their investment strategy to align with their unique circumstances.

ECONOMICS | TRIENT PRESS

TRIENT PRESS MAGAZINE FEBRUARY/ MARCH

Active vs. Passive Investing

Active and passive investing strategies have their merit. Active investors seek to capitalize on market inefficiencies through hands-on management, while passive investors opt for low-cost index funds of Exchange-Traded Funds (ETFs). The choice between the two should reflect an investor's objectives and risk tolerance.

Technological Advancements and Digital Assets

The digital age has ushered in a new era of investment opportunities, including cryptocurrencies and blockchain technology. While these assets offer diversification potential, they also carry increased volatility and regulatory uncertainties. Investors should approach digital assets with caution and seek expert guidance.

Sustainable and ESG Investments

Sustainable and Environmental, Social, and Governance (ESG) investments are gaining prominence. Companies that prioritize sustainability and ethical practices are attracting investor interest. Integrating ESG considerations into an investment strategy aligns with both financial goals and responsible investing principles.

Long-Term vs. Short-Term Vision

Investors often grapple with the choice between short-term gains and long-term stability. A balanced approach that combines short-term liquidity needs with a long-term vision can help weather economic uncertainty while preserving capital growth opportunities.

ECONOMICS | TRIENT PRESS

> "The digital age has ushered in a new era of investment opportunities, including cryptocurrencies and blockchain technology."

Seeking Expert Guidance

In turbulent times, seeking advice from financial experts is invaluable. Wealth managers, financial advisors, and investment professionals provide insights, conduct risk assessments, and tailor strategies to individual financial objectives. Their expertise can help investors make well-informed decisions.

Staying Informed and Adaptive

Economic landscapes are dynamic, and successful investors stay informed and adaptive. Monitoring market trends, economic indicators, and global events allows investors to adjust their strategies as circumstances evolve.

Navigating the Road Ahead

In conclusion, the world of investing, the road ahead is never without twists and turns. Economic uncertainty is an inevitable part of the journey, but it need not be an insurmountable challenge. Informed investment strategies, risk assessment, diversification, and expert guidance are the navigational tools that empower investors to thrive in turbulent times.

As we confront the uncertainties of the global economic landscape in 2024, it's important to remember that challenges also bring opportunities. Informed investors, armed with knowledge and adaptability, can seize these opportunities and build resilient portfolios that weather the storms and capitalize on the calms.

In the end, navigating economic uncertainty is not just about safeguarding wealth; it's about steering toward financial prosperity amid the ever-changing currents of the global economy.

Trient Press

THE ULTIMATE FINANCIAL MASTERY PROGRAM

DATE
April 3, 2024

BENEFITS OF THE PROGRAM

Unlock Your Financial Potential!

🚀 Join 'The Ultimate Financial Mastery Program' and supercharge your financial journey. Discover the secrets to mastering both personal and business finances while expanding your professional network.

⭐ Invaluable Insights: Unearth the hidden treasures of financial management. Gain practical knowledge that will revolutionize your financial strategy.

🌐 Transform Your Perspective: See finances from a new angle. This course will reshape the way you think about money, creating a path to prosperity.

🤝 Network with Success: Connect with like-minded individuals and experts in the field. Forge partnerships that can change your financial destiny.

Don't miss this opportunity! Enroll now and embark on a transformative financial adventure. Your financial success story begins here.

Melisa Ruscsak
Trainer

MORE INFO
📞 775-249-7401

TRIENT PRESS MAGAZINE　　　　　FEBRUARY/ MARCH

THE RISE OF GREEN ECONOMICS:
HOW SUSTAINABLE PRACTICES ARE SHAPING MARKETS

Impact on Investment and Finance

The rise of green economics has far-reaching implications for the world of finance and investment. Sustainable investing, often known as Environmental, Social, and Governance (ESG) investing, is on the ascent. Investors are directing capital toward companies that align with sustainability goals, recognizing that these businesses are better positioned for long-term success.

Government Policies and Green Stimulus

Governments worldwide are implementing policies and incentives to promote green initiatives. From renewable energy subsidies to carbon pricing mechanisms, these policies are reshaping industries and accelerating the transition to a low-carbon economy. Green stimulus packages, such as investments in clean infrastructure and renewable energy projects, are also boosting economic growth while advancing sustainability goals.

In an era defined by environmental awareness and a growing commitment to combating climate change, the world of economics is undergoing a profound transformation. Sustainable practices and the principles of "green economics" are not only shaping industries but also redefining the way we approach business and finance. As we stand on the precipice of a more sustainable future, it's evident that the green revolution is not just an ethical choice; it's a strategic imperative that is redefining markets worldwide.

The Emergence of Green Economics

Green economics, often referred to as ecological economics, is a discipline that integrates environmental considerations into economic policy and decision-making. Its emergence is driven by a recognition that the traditional model of economic growth, which often leads to resource depletion and environmental degradation, is unsustainable in the long run.

Sustainable Practices and Corporate Responsibility

One of the key drivers of green economics is the corporate world's increasing emphasis on sustainability. Companies are no longer viewed solely through the lens of profit; they are also evaluated based on their environmental and social impact. Sustainable practices, including carbon reduction initiatives, waste reduction, and responsible sourcing, have become integral components of corporate responsibility.

ECONOMICS |TRIENT PRESS

TRIENT PRESS MAGAZINE   FEBRUARY/ MARCH

➡ The Circular Economy and Resource Efficiency

A fundamental tenet of green economics is the concept of the circular economy. This approach aims to minimize waste and maximize the reuse, recycling, and repurposing of resources. Businesses that adopt circular economy principles not only reduce their environmental footprint but also benefit from cost savings and enhanced resource efficiency.

➡ Global Supply Chains and Responsible Sourcing

The globalization of supply chains has brought greater scrutiny to the sourcing of materials and products. Responsible sourcing practices, such as ensuring ethical labor conditions and sustainable resource extraction, are becoming prerequisites for businesses that aim to remain competitive in global markets.

➡ Consumer Demand and Ethical Consumption

Consumers are increasingly making purchasing decisions based on ethical and sustainability considerations. This shift in consumer demand is driving companies to prioritize eco-friendly products and responsible production methods. Brands that fail to adapt risk losing market share.

CONCLUSION: A SUSTAINABLE FUTURE

The rise of green economics signals a new era in which sustainability is no longer an option but a necessity. Businesses, investors, governments, and consumers are recognizing that a sustainable future is not only ecologically responsible but also economically viable.

As we witness the transformation of industries and markets under the banner of green economics, it's clear that sustainability is not just a trend; it's a defining feature of the global economic landscape. Embracing sustainability is not only a moral imperative but also a strategic choice that positions businesses and economies for resilience and long-term success.

In the journey toward a more sustainable future, green economics is not merely a destination; it's the compass guiding us toward a world where economic prosperity is harmoniously intertwined with environmental stewardship.

ECONOMICS | TRIENT PRESS

Emerging Markets in 2024:
Risks and Rewards for International Investors

Emerging markets have long held the allure of untapped potential, offering international investors the promise of high returns and exciting growth opportunities.

However, they also come with their fair share of risks and uncertainties. As we enter the year 2024, the landscape of emerging markets is evolving, presenting both challenges and rewards for those willing to navigate these dynamic and diverse economies.

THE SHIFTING LANDSCAPE OF EMERGING MARKETS

Emerging markets encompass a wide range of economies, each at a different stage of development. In 2024, several trends and factors are shaping the landscape of these markets:

ECONOMICS | TRIENT PRESS

Digital Transformation:
Many emerging markets are experiencing rapid digital transformation, with increased internet penetration, e-commerce growth, and the adoption of digital payment systems. This presents opportunities for technology and e-commerce investors.

Sustainability Focus:
Sustainability and ESG considerations are gaining prominence in emerging markets. Companies that embrace sustainability practices are attracting investment, reflecting global trends.

Geopolitical Uncertainties:
Geopolitical tensions can impact emerging markets significantly. Investors must assess the geopolitical risks associated with each market and consider diversification.

Infrastructure Investment:
Infrastructure development remains a priority in many emerging markets, creating opportunities in sectors such as transportation, energy, and telecommunications.

Consumer Markets:
Rising middle-class populations in emerging markets present opportunities for consumer goods and services companies. However, consumer preferences and market dynamics can vary widely.

TRIENT PRESS MAGAZINE   FEBRUARY/ MARCH

RISKS AND REWARDS FOR INTERNATIONAL INVESTORS

For international investors eyeing emerging markets in 2024, here's a closer look at the risks and rewards:

REWARDS:

High Growth Potential:
Emerging markets often outpace developed economies in terms of economic growth. Investors can benefit from the potential for higher returns on investments.

Diversification:
Investing in emerging markets provides diversification benefits, reducing the correlation with developed markets and potentially enhancing portfolio risk-adjusted returns.

Untapped Markets:
Emerging markets offer access to large populations and growing consumer markets. Companies that can tap into these markets can achieve substantial growth.

Innovation and Technology:
Emerging markets are hubs of innovation and technology adoption. Investors can capitalize on the growth of tech startups and digital businesses.

RISKS:

Political and Regulatory Risks:
Political instability and regulatory uncertainties can pose significant challenges. Investors must stay informed about the political landscape in each market.

Currency Volatility:
Currency fluctuations can affect returns for international investors. Hedging strategies may be necessary to mitigate currency risk.

Liquidity Concerns:
Some emerging markets may have lower liquidity and transparency levels, making it harder to execute large trades and assess investment risks.

Economic Vulnerabilities:
Emerging markets can be vulnerable to economic crises, including currency crises and financial market turbulence. Prudent risk management is crucial.

NAVIGATING THE EMERGING MARKETS LANDSCAPE

Emerging markets offer a tantalizing blend of risks and rewards for international investors. Success in these markets requires a comprehensive understanding of the specific economic, political, and regulatory factors in play in each region.

In 2024, as emerging markets continue to evolve, investors should approach them with a well-informed and diversified strategy. Thorough due diligence, risk assessment, and a long-term perspective can help international investors unlock the potential rewards while mitigating the associated risks.

As the global economy becomes increasingly interconnected, emerging markets remain a pivotal part of the investment landscape. For those willing to embark on this dynamic journey, the year 2024 holds the promise of exciting opportunities and potential for growth in these diverse and evolving economies.

TRADE WARS to TRADE WINS

THE FUTURE OF INTERNATIONAL TRADE AGREEMENT

The world of international trade has witnessed its fair share of turbulence in recent years, characterized by trade wars, tariff disputes, and economic tensions. However, as we look ahead to the future of international trade agreements, there are signs of a shifting tide. The once murky waters of conflict are giving way to a new era of collaboration and the potential for trade wins that can benefit economies and businesses worldwide.

THE TRADE WARS ERA

The early 21st century will be remembered for the trade wars that dominated global headlines. Trade disputes between major economic powers, such as the United States and China, led to tit-for-tat tariffs and raised concerns about the stability of the international trading system. The resulting uncertainty cast a shadow over global commerce.

THE SHIFT TOWARDS COOPERATION

In recent years, there has been a noticeable shift towards cooperation and a renewed commitment to multilateralism in international trade. Several factors are contributing to this change:

Global Challenges:
The COVID-19 pandemic highlighted the interdependence of nations and the importance of cooperation in addressing global challenges, including healthcare and supply chain resilience.

Climate Change:
The urgency of addressing climate change has led to discussions about trade policies that support sustainability and green technologies.

Digitalization:
The rise of digital trade and e-commerce has prompted the need for international rules that facilitate cross-border digital transactions.

Technological Innovation:
Emerging technologies, such as blockchain and artificial intelligence, are reshaping industries and trade practices, requiring international agreements to adapt.

ECONOMICS | TRIENT PRESS

KEY DEVELOPMENTS AND OPPORTUNITIES

In the evolving landscape of international trade agreements, several key developments and opportunities are worth noting:

The Reinvigoration of the WTO:

Efforts are underway to reform the World Trade Organization (WTO) and strengthen its role as a forum for resolving trade disputes and setting global trade rules.

Regional Trade Agreements:

Regional trade agreements, such as the Comprehensive and Progressive Agreement for Trans-Pacific Partnership (CPTPP), are gaining momentum and offering new opportunities for trade expansion.

Digital Trade Agreements:

The negotiation of agreements related to digital trade and data governance is becoming increasingly important in the digital age.

Sustainability and ESG Considerations:

Trade agreements are increasingly incorporating sustainability and Environmental, Social, and Governance (ESG) principles, reflecting the global focus on responsible business practices.

THE PATH TO TRADE WINS

The future of international trade agreements holds promise for trade wins that can benefit economies and businesses worldwide. To navigate this path successfully, stakeholders must consider the following:

COLLABORATION AND DIPLOMACY:
Nations must prioritize collaboration and diplomacy to resolve trade disputes and promote international cooperation.

ADAPTABILITY:
International trade agreements must be adaptable to accommodate technological advancements and emerging industries.

SUSTAINABILITY:
Sustainability and ESG considerations should be integral to trade agreements, aligning economic growth with environmental and social responsibility.

INCLUSIVITY:
Inclusivity is key, ensuring that trade agreements benefit a broad spectrum of industries and economies.

A NEW ERA OF TRADE

The future of international trade agreements offers hope for a new era of trade characterized by cooperation, innovation, and sustainability. As economies recover from the challenges of recent years, the potential for trade wins that benefit nations and businesses alike becomes increasingly evident.

While the path ahead may still have its share of challenges, the overarching trend toward collaboration and the pursuit of mutually beneficial trade agreements signals a positive shift in the international trade landscape. The era of trade wars is gradually giving way to an era of trade wins that can shape a more prosperous and interconnected global economy.

PATH BENDER

By: Antonio T. Smith, Jr

HARDCOVER PRICE: $29.99

FIGHTING FOR MY LIFE TO WIN (PAPERBACK)

By: Arshisa Adejiyan

PRICE: $16.99

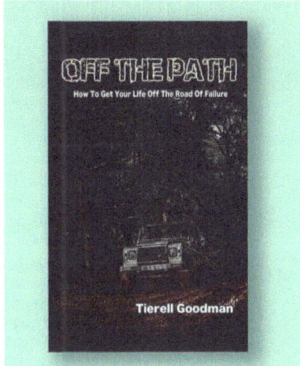

OFF THE PATH (PAPERBACK)

By: Tierell Goodman

PRICE: $24.99

RESILIENT SAILING (PAPERBACK)

By: Dr Carl M Barnes

PRICE: $28.26

NATURE'S PHARMACY : UNLOCKING THE POWER OF MEDICINAL HERBS

By: Deaunna M Smith

PRICE: $32.99

ARE YOU HAPPY : FINDING THE CEO IN YOU (HARDCOVER)

By: M.L.Ruscsak

PRICE: $29.99

Embracing the Serenity: A moment of mindfulness in the midst of nature, brought to you by Trient Press – nurturing your mindset, one page at a time.

+1 -775-249-7401

info@trientperess.com
www.trientpress.com

TRIENT PRESS MAGAZINE FEBRUARY/ MARCH

Technological Innovations:
Shaping the Future of Business

Trient Press Staff Writer

The business world has always been characterized by evolution and adaptation, but in the 21st century, the pace of change has reached unprecedented levels. At the heart of this transformation are technological innovations that are not only reshaping industries but also redefining the very essence of how businesses operate and compete. As we embark on this journey into the future of business, it's clear that technology is the compass guiding us towards uncharted territories of possibility and potential.

THE TECHNOLOGICAL REVOLUTION

The advent of the digital age has ushered in a technological revolution that has left no industry untouched. The confluence of technologies such as artificial intelligence, data analytics, cloud computing, and the Internet of Things has created a powerful force that is propelling businesses into uncharted territory.

DATA: THE NEW CURRENCY

In the digital era, data has emerged as the new currency of business. Companies are now able to collect, analyze, and leverage vast amounts of data to gain insights into customer behavior, streamline operations, and make data-driven decisions. This data-driven approach is transforming the way businesses understand and serve their markets.

ARTIFICIAL INTELLIGENCE AND AUTOMATION

Artificial intelligence (AI) is revolutionizing everything from customer service to supply chain management. Machine learning algorithms can analyze vast datasets to make predictions and automate processes, leading to increased efficiency and cost savings.

E-COMMERCE AND DIGITAL TRANSFORMATION

[E-]commerce has become the lifeblood of retail, with [con]sumers increasingly turning to online platforms for their [sho]pping needs. The digital transformation of businesses [inc]ludes the development of user-friendly websites, mobile [app]s, and seamless online shopping experiences.

CYBERSECURITY AND DIGITAL TRUST

[As] businesses rely more heavily on digital technologies, the [im]portance of cybersecurity cannot be overstated. [Pro]tecting customer data and maintaining digital trust has [bec]ome paramount, and businesses are investing heavily in [cyb]ersecurity measures.

REMOTE WORK AND THE GIG ECONOMY

[Tec]hnological innovations have also reshaped the [wo]rkforce. Remote work and the gig economy are [bec]oming more prevalent, offering flexibility for workers [and] cost savings for businesses. Collaboration tools and [rem]ote work technologies are now essential for many [org]anizations.

SUSTAINABILITY AND GREEN TECHNOLOGIES

[Inn]ovations in green technologies are driving sustainability [eff]orts. Businesses are increasingly adopting renewable [en]ergy sources, implementing energy-efficient practices, [and] exploring sustainable materials and production [me]thods.

While technological innovations offer boundless opportunities, they also present challenges:

- **Rapid Change:** Businesses must adapt quickly to keep pace with technological advancements, requiring a culture of continuous learning and innovation.

- **Cybersecurity Threats:** The increasing reliance on technology exposes businesses to cybersecurity threats that can be financially and reputationally damaging.

- **Ethical Considerations:** The use of AI and data raises ethical questions about privacy, bias, and accountability that businesses must address.

- **Competition:** The global reach of technology means increased competition from both domestic and international players.

In the ever-evolving landscape of business, technology is the driving force that is shaping not only what we do but also how we do it. As businesses navigate this era of innovation, embracing technology is not an option; it's a strategic imperative. The future belongs to those who can harness the power of technological innovations to create value, drive efficiency, and meet the evolving needs of their customers.

As we look to the horizon of business, it's evident that the compass guiding us forward is marked with the coordinates of technology. The future of business is a landscape where innovation is not just a choice it's the essence of survival and success. It's a world where businesses that embrace technological innovations will not only thrive but also shape the course of industries, economies, and societies.

TECHNOLOGY |TRIENT PRESS

MICA BEAUTY

UNLEASH YOUR TRUE BEAUTY WITH MICABEAUTY - WHERE EVERY SHADE IS CELEBRATED!

Discover Your Perfect Match: Dive into the world of MicaBeauty, where we embrace every skin tone with our inclusive and personalized beauty range. From radiant foundations to luscious lip balms, our non-toxic, harsh chemical-free products are crafted for your unique beauty.

Be Part of Our Story: Join us on a journey of beauty that defies norms. At MicaBeauty, we're more than just a brand; we're a community that celebrates the real you.

https://shrsl.com/4cp62

> TapJoy · Mica Beauty Cosmetics & Skincare Products

GLOW GETTER VALUE KIT

$175.00 ~~$210.00~~

or 4 interest-free payments of $43.75 with afterpay

6-piece full size skincare products + mini fridge

Note: Kits are not available internationally

Special Offer: Enjoy free shipping on U.S. orders over $50! Plus, get a FREE mini fridge with purchases over $100*

ARTIFICIAL INTELLIGENCE IN THE WORKPLACE: ENHANCING EFFICIENCY OR DISPLACING JOBS?

Artificial intelligence (AI) has emerged as a transformative force in the workplace, promising to enhance efficiency, productivity, and innovation. However, as AI technologies become increasingly integrated into business operations, questions arise about their impact on the workforce. Are AI systems enhancing efficiency or displacing jobs? Let's delve into this complex and evolving landscape.

AI technologies encompass a range of capabilities, from natural language processing and machine learning to robotics and automation. In the workplace, AI holds the potential to revolutionize various aspects of business operations:

Enhanced Efficiency: AI-powered tools can automate routine tasks, allowing employees to focus on higher-value activities. This can lead to increased productivity and cost savings.

Data Analysis: AI systems can analyze vast datasets in real time, providing valuable insights for decision-making and strategy development.

Personalization: AI enables personalized customer experiences, from chatbots that assist customers to recommendation engines that tailor product offerings.

Predictive Maintenance: In manufacturing and logistics, AI can predict equipment maintenance needs, reducing downtime and improving operational efficiency.

Innovation: AI fosters innovation by enabling businesses to develop new products, services, and business models.

JOB DISPLACEMENT CONCERNS

While the potential benefits of AI in the workplace are clear, concerns about job displacement persist:

- Automation of Routine Tasks: Jobs that involve repetitive and routine tasks are susceptible to automation, potentially leading to job displacement for certain roles.

- Skill Mismatch: As AI systems become more integral, there may be a gap between the skills required for emerging roles and the skills possessed by the existing workforce.

- Change Management: Implementing AI technologies may require significant changes in workflow and job roles, which can be challenging for employees and organizations.

- Ethical Considerations: AI raises ethical questions about transparency, accountability, and bias in decision-making, which need to be addressed.

TECHNOLOGY | TRIENT PRESS

BALANCING EFFICIENCY AND EMPLOYMENT

The key challenge lies in striking a balance between harnessing the efficiency-enhancing potential of AI and preserving jobs. Here are strategies to achieve this balance:

- Reskilling and Upskilling: Invest in employee training and development to ensure that the workforce is equipped with the skills needed to collaborate effectively with AI systems.

- Redesigning Roles: Redefine job roles to complement AI capabilities. Employees can focus on tasks that require creativity, critical thinking, empathy, and complex problem-solving.

- Ethical AI: Implement AI systems with a strong ethical framework, ensuring transparency, fairness, and accountability in decision-making processes.

- Change Management: Manage the transition to AI technology through effective change management practices that engage and support employees.

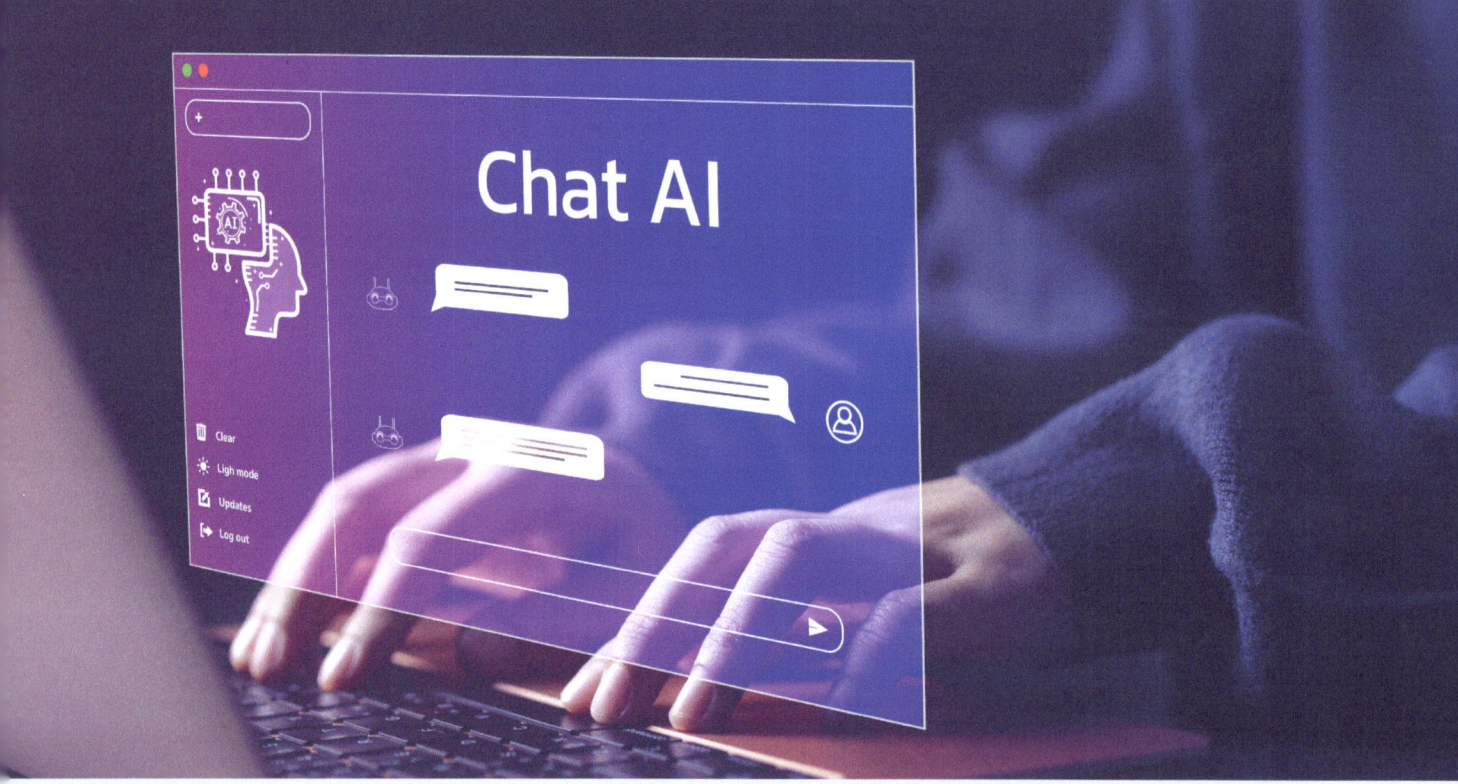

AI in the workplace is not a binary choice between enhancing efficiency and displacing jobs. Rather, it represents a transformation of work, with the potential to augment human capabilities, drive innovation, and improve business outcomes. However, achieving this potential requires a proactive approach that combines technology integration with workforce development and ethical considerations.

The future of work is a dynamic landscape where humans and AI coexist, each contributing their unique strengths to create more efficient, productive, and innovative workplace. The path forward is not without challenges, but with strategic planning and commitment to responsible AI deployment, organizations can harness the full potential of artificial intelligence while ensuring that it benefits both business and society.

The Next Frontier

How Quantum Computing is Transforming Industries

In the realm of computing, a new frontier is unfolding—one that promises to revolutionize industries and reshape the boundaries of what is possible. Quantum computing, with its immense computational power and ability to solve complex problems previously deemed insurmountable, is poised to transform industries across the spectrum. In this article, we delve into the profound impact of quantum computing on various sectors of the economy.

QUANTUM COMPUTING UNVEILED

At its core, quantum computing harnesses the principles of quantum mechanics to perform calculations at speeds that defy the capabilities of classical computers. Unlike classical bits, which can represent either a 0 or a 1, quantum bits or qubits can exist in multiple states simultaneously through a phenomenon called superposition. This inherent parallelism makes quantum computers exceptionally powerful for tackling complex tasks.

APPLICATIONS ACROSS INDUSTRIES

- Pharmaceuticals and Drug Discovery:
Quantum computing accelerates drug discovery by simulating molecular interactions with unparalleled precision. It enables researchers to explore a vast chemical space, leading to the development of new drugs and therapies.

- Finance and Optimization:
In the financial sector, quantum computing can optimize portfolios, model risk more accurately, and solve complex financial equations. This has implications for trading strategies, risk management, and fraud detection.

- Materials Science and Manufacturing:
Quantum computing aids in the design of advanced materials with specific properties, revolutionizing materials science and manufacturing processes. This includes creating stronger, lighter materials for aerospace and automotive industries.

- Supply Chain and Logistics:
Quantum computing optimizes supply chain and logistics operations by solving complex routing and scheduling processes. problems, leading to cost savings and more efficient delivery.

- Energy and Sustainability:
Quantum computing is instrumental in solving complex optimization problems related to renewable energy generation, grid management, and resource allocation, contributing to a more sustainable future.

- Artificial Intelligence and Machine Learning:
Quantum computing enhances machine learning algorithms, enabling faster training of AI models and the exploration of new AI architectures.

CHALLENGES AND CONSIDERATIONS

While the potential of quantum computing is immense, there are challenges to overcome:

- Hardware Development:
Building and maintaining stable quantum hardware remains a significant challenge. Researchers are continually working to improve qubit stability and error correction.

> "Quantum computing, with its immense computational power and ability to solve complex problems previously deemed insurmountable, is poised to transform industries across the spectrum."

- Security:
Quantum computers also pose threat to cybersecurity as they can potentially break widely-us encryption methods. This has prompted the development of quantum-resistant encryption.

- Skills Gap:
There is a shortage of quantum computing experts. Addressing this gap through education and training is crucial to realizing t technology's full potential.

In summary, Quantum computing represents a quantu leap forward in computational capabilities. Its transformative impact extends to industries as diverse as healthcare, finance, materials science, and logistics. However, the journey into the quantum frontier is not withou its challenges.

Businesses and governments worldwide are investing in quantum research and development to harness its potential. As quantum computing matures, it will not only optimize existing processe but also unlock new frontiers o discovery and innovation. The quantum age is dawning, and those who embrace this technological leap will lead the way into a future where the impossible becomes possible.

TRIENT PRESS MAGAZINE   FEBRUARY/ MARCH

BLOCKCHAIN BEYOND CRYPTOCURRENCY:
REAL-WORLD BUSINESS APPLICATIONS

BLOCKCHAIN TECHNOLOGY, ORIGINALLY DESIGNED TO UNDERPIN CRYPTOCURRENCIES LIKE BITCOIN, HAS TRANSCENDED ITS INITIAL PURPOSE. BEYOND THE REALM OF DIGITAL CURRENCIES, BLOCKCHAIN IS EMERGING AS A TRANSFORMATIVE FORCE IN THE BUSINESS WORLD, OFFERING SOLUTIONS TO A MYRIAD OF CHALLENGES. IN THIS ARTICLE, WE EXPLORE THE DIVERSE APPLICATIONS OF BLOCKCHAIN TECHNOLOGY IN VARIOUS SECTORS OF THE BUSINESS LANDSCAPE.

THE FOUNDATION OF BLOCKCHAIN

At its core, blockchain is a distributed ledger technology that enables secure, transparent, and tamper-proof recording of transactions. Data is stored in blocks, and each block is linked to the previous one, creating an unbroken chain. This design ensures data immutability and integrity, making blockchain a powerful tool for trust and accountability.

TECHNOLOGY | TRIENT PRESS

TRIENT PRESS MAGAZINE   FEBRUARY/ MARCH

Applications Across Industries

Supply Chain Management: Blockchain provides end-to-end visibility in supply chains. It enables tracking of goods from origin to destination, reducing fraud, ensuring product authenticity, and optimizing logistics.

- Financial Services: Beyond cryptocurrency, blockchain simplifi cross-border payments, reduces transaction costs, and enhances transparency in financial transactions. Smart contracts automate and enforce agreements.
- Healthcare: In healthcare, blockchain secures patient records, streamlines data sharing among providers, and enables patients to have control over their health data while ensuring privacy.
- Real Estate: Blockchain simplifies property transactions, reducing fraud in real estate deals. It also allows for fractional ownership of properties, opening up investment opportunities.
- Intellectual Property: Artists, writers, and creators can use blockchain to timestamp and protect their intellectual propert ensuring copyright protection.
- Voting Systems: Blockchain-based voting systems enhance th integrity of elections, providing transparent and secure voting processes.
- Smart Cities: Blockchain can facilitate the development of sm cities by managing and securing data from IoT devices, optimizing energy consumption, and improving urban services
- Food Safety: In the food industry, blockchain can trace the orig of products, enabling rapid recalls in case of contamination ar ensuring food safety.

Challenges and Considerations:

While blockchain offers diverse benefits, challenges persist.

<u>Scalability:</u> Scaling blockchain networks to handle a high volume of transactions is a technical challenge that continues to be addressed.

<u>Regulatory Frameworks:</u> The regulatory landscape for blockchain varies by jurisdiction, <u>creating</u> compliance complexities.

<u>Interoperability:</u> Ensuring that different blockchain platforms can communicate seamlessly is crucial for widespread adoption.

<u>Energy Consumption:</u> Some blockchain networks, like Bitcoin, consume significant energy. Sustainability concerns are prompting exploration of greener alternatives.

Blockchain technology unlocks the potential and transcends its origins in cryptocurrency, offering a versatile toolkit for businesses across industries. Its applications span from supply chain management to healthcare, real estate, and beyond. While challenges exist, the potential for increased transparency, efficiency, and trust in business processes is undeniable.

As businesses continue to explore and adopt blockchain solutions, they are laying the foundation for a future where trust and security are not just aspirations but fundamental attributes of the digital age. Blockchain's diverse applications promise to reshape industries, drive innovation, and empower individuals and organizations to take control of their data and transactions.

WINTER
Sale
DON'T MISS IT!

HTTPS://SHRSL.COM/4CP6O

TRIENT PRESS MAGAZINE — FEBRUARY/ MARCH

Cybersecurity in 2024

Safeguarding Your Business in the Digital Era

Trient Press Staff Writer

In the intricate tapestry of the digital age, the year 2024 emerges as a pivotal juncture where businesses navigate the crossroads of innovation and security. The relentless march of technology presents a multitude of opportunities, but it also unfurls a treacherous landscape of cyber threats. In this imperative discourse, we unveil the indispensable strategies and insights that will empower enterprises to not only withstand the digital tempest but also flourish with unwavering trust and resilience.

THE VAST EXPANSE OF VULNERABILITY

In an age characterized by ceaseless connectivity, the periphery of vulnerability has expanded to an unprecedented scale. The Internet of Things (IoT), cloud ecosystems, and the paradigm of remote work have catalyzed an astronomical growth in the attack surface. This demands, more than ever, a ceaseless vigil against imminent risks.

THE SHIFTING PANORAMA OF THREATS

As the year 2024 unfolds, one must recognize that the threat spectrum is no longer confined to conventional malware or rudimentary phishing ploys. The evolving threat panorama boasts sophisticated Advanced Persistent Threats (APTs), insidious ransomware assaults, supply chain intricacies, and even nation-state-backed cyber-espionage. Perpetrators of cyber threats have honed their craft to a fine art, necessitating a correspondingly sophisticated defense.

TECHNOLOGY | TRIENT PRESS

The Imperatives of Cybersecurity in 2024

Zero Trust Paradigm: Embrace the Zero Trust framework, where trust is never a presumption but an ongoing validation. This mandates perpetual authentication, stringent access control, and meticulous network segmentation.

Artificial Intelligence and Machine Learning: Leverage the supremacy of artificial intelligence and machine learning to discern anomalies and decipher patterns indicative of cyber perils. These potent technologies are your arsenal for proactive threat identification and swift counteraction.

Endpoint Fortification: Fortify your endpoints with state-of-the-art antivirus software, Endpoint Detection and Response (EDR) systems, and robust vulnerability management. Remember, endpoint security extends beyond traditional endpoints to encompass the burgeoning universe of IoT devices.

Cloud Guardian: Safeguard your cloud environments with unwavering Identity and Access Management (IAM), encryption protocols, and recurrent security evaluations. Equip yourself with cloud-native security solutions to shield data and applications housed in the cloud.

Human Capital Training: Cybersecurity education is not a mere formality; it's your bulwark against cyber invasions. Enrich your workforce with regular training initiatives, molding them into sentinels capable of recognizing and thwarting sophisticated threats.

Incident Handling and Resilience: Construct and meticulously test your incident response blueprints. Timely response and swift recovery are quintessential in minimizing the repercussions of cyber incidents.

Supply Chain Safeguarding: Delve into the intricacies of your supply chain. Identify vulnerabilities and secure your critical vendors to prevent potential disruptions stemming from supply chain attacks.

THE CRUCIBLE OF REGULATORY COMPLIANCE

In the epoch of data privacy and heightened cybersecurity consciousness, adherence to rigorous regulatory mandates is an inescapable commitment. Familiarize yourself with formidable data protection regulations such as GDPR, CCPA, and the burgeoning legislative framework. Ensure your cybersecurity posture aligns seamlessly with these regulatory imperatives.

In this epoch-defining odyssey into the digital frontier of 2024, the essence of cybersecurity transcends the peripheries of technological adaptation. It emerges as an elemental business necessity—a vanguard shielding against the digital maelstrom. Cyber threats, dynamic and unrelenting, compel organizations to assimilate cybersecurity as a fundamental business doctrine.

The year 2024 unveils a cyber landscape demanding nothing short of an all-encompassing strategy. In this endeavor, technology converges with human ingenuity and a zealous commitment to perpetual betterment. Safeguarding your business in the digital age is not a mere protocol; it is a ceaseless voyage, demanding unwavering vigilance, adaptability, and a proactive stance against the inexorable evolution of digital threats.

In this era of transformative digitalization, wherein the demarcation between the tangible and the virtual fades, cybersecurity assumes the mantle of both safeguard and enabler. It is the assurance of a resilient digital realm—a realm where possibilities are boundless, and risks are not only mitigated but transcended with precision and expertise. This is the definitive guide to securing your enterprise in the digital age of 2024—a must-read testament to your commitment to a future of prosperity, trust, and technological ascendancy.

TECHNOLOGY | TRIENT PRESS

TRIENT PRESS MAGAZINE — FEBRUARY/MARCH

The Impact of 5G Technology

BUSINESS OPERATIONS & CONSUMER BEHAVIOR

In the tapestry of technological advancements, few threads have woven as transformative a narrative as the advent of 5G technology. As we stand at the cusp of a new era, the repercussions of 5G are poised to reverberate far beyond the realm of telecommunications. In this discourse, we delve into the profound impact of 5G technology on both the fabric of business operations and the intricacies of consumer behavior.

THE UNVEILING OF 5G

5G, the fifth generation of wireless technology, transcends the boundaries of mere connectivity. With its promise of lightning-fast speeds, ultra-low latency, and the ability to support a multitude of connected devices simultaneously, it is a technological quantum leap. Its impact extends across a spectrum of industries and spheres of life, heralding an era of unprecedented possibilities.

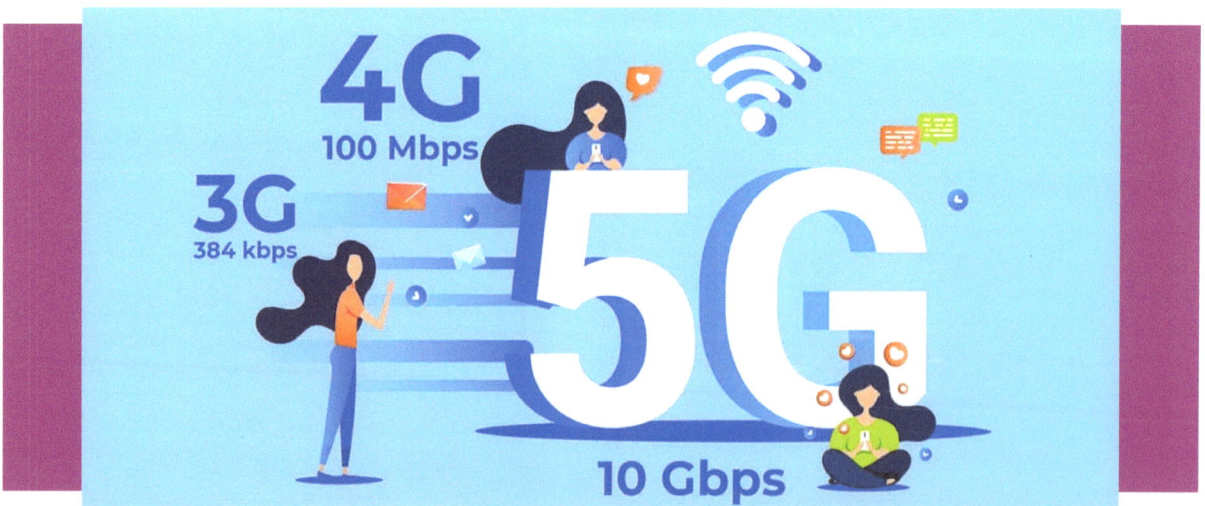

REIMAGINING BUSINESS OPERATIONS:

- **Enhanced Connectivity:** The most immediate transformation is perhaps in business operations. 5G's high-speed, low-latency connectivity is a game-changer. It fuels seamless communication, enabling remote work to reach new heights of efficiency. In industries reliant on real-time data, such as manufacturing and logistics, 5G paves the way for enhanced automation and operational agility.

- **IoT Revolution:** The Internet of Things (IoT) blossoms in the fertile ground of 5G. Industries from healthcare to agriculture leverage 5G's capacity to connect a multitude of devices. Smart cities materialize, with real-time data facilitating intelligent traffic management, energy conservation, and enhanced public services.

- **Augmented Reality (AR) and Virtual Reality (VR):** AR and VR technologies, hitherto constrained by bandwidth limitations, are set for a renaissance. Industries like healthcare employ AR for remote surgeries, while retail explores VR for immersive shopping experiences. Employee training becomes a dynamic arena, with simulations and training modules harnessing the power of 5G.

- **Supply Chain Revolution:** Supply chains undergo a renaissance, with real-time tracking and predictive analytics powered by 5G. Businesses benefit from enhanced visibility, reduced lead times, and increased resilience against disruptions.

- **Content Delivery:** Media and entertainment industries seize the opportunity to deliver high-definition content seamlessly, opening doors for interactive and immersive experiences. Live streaming, augmented sports viewing, and interactive storytelling redefine the entertainment landscape.

THE IMPACT OF 5G ON CONSUMER BEHAVIOR IS EQUALLY PROFOUND:

Instant Gratification: The age of waiting for content to load is fading into oblivion. Consumers now expect instant access to information, entertainment, and services. This demand for immediacy influences everything from online shopping to content consumption.

Immersive Experiences: Consumers crave immersive experiences, and 5G delivers. AR and VR applications offer immersive gaming, virtual travel, and interactive shopping, creating new avenues for consumer engagement.

IoT Adoption: Smart homes become smarter, with interconnected devices offering convenience and efficiency. Consumers embrace IoT devices for security, energy management, and enhanced living experiences.

Telemedicine: The healthcare landscape transforms as telemedicine gains prominence. Patients seek remote consultations and health monitoring, empowered by 5G's robust connectivity.

Retail Revolution: Retailers leverage 5G for cashierless stores, augmented reality try-ons, and personalized shopping experiences. Consumers benefit from enhanced convenience and tailored offerings.

In summation, as 5G technology unfurls its transformative potential, it ushers in an inflection point for both business and consumers. Business operations evolve into agile, data-driven ecosystems, while consumers embark on a journey of instant gratification and immersive experiences. The 5G era is not just about connectivity; it's a metamorphosis of how we work, play, and interact.

For businesses, embracing 5G is not a choice but a necessity to remain competitive in an increasingly digital landscape. For consumers, the 5G era is a promise of seamless experiences, offering a glimpse into a future where the boundaries of possibility continue to expand. As we stand on the precipice of this transformative era, one thing is certain: the impact of 5G technology will redefine the dynamics of business and consumer behavior in ways that we are only beginning to fathom.

Traveling with Trient

TRAVEL TIPS
AND A TASTE OF THE CITY

WWW.TRIENTPRESSMAGAZINE.COM

UNVEILING THE WONDERS OF YBNB:

"A JOURNEY TO REMEMBER"

BY M.L. RUSCSAK

Picture this: A crystal clear evening in San Diego, California. A vibrant gathering of travel enthusiasts, brimming with tales of adventures and the promise of new discoveries. This is precisely the atmosphere I was immersed in at the 2023 event for 'Your Best Night's Bed' (YBNB) - a platform revolutionizing the way we experience travel.

As a passionate traveler and advocate for unique experiences, attending this event was akin to stepping into a realm where every conversation opened the door to a world of possibilities. YBNB, with its innovative approach, is redefining what it means to travel and stay in comfort.

Let me walk you through this experience, almost as if you were there with me, mingling among fellow globetrotters and sharing stories that span continents. The energy at the event was palpable - a blend of excitement, curiosity, and a shared love for exploration. YBNB has created not just a service, but a community where travel stories are currency, and every member is both a storyteller and an eager listener.

What sets YBNB apart is its commitment to providing not just a place to stay, but an experience to cherish. Imagine waking up in a cozy bed in a foreign land, feeling not like a tourist, but a local, thanks to the unique accommodations and authentic experiences curated by YBNB. This platform is more than just a booking site; it's a gateway to living and breathing the culture of your destination.

The highlight of the event was the sheer diversity of experiences shared by YBNB users. From a quaint cottage in the Scottish Highlands to a modern apartment in the heart of Tokyo, YBNB's portfolio is as diverse as it is exciting. It's not just about the place; it's about the experience - the local cuisine, the hidden trails, the cultural immersion.

As I engaged in conversations, what struck me was the enthusiasm of YBNB users in sharing their adventures. It was like a grand exchange of hidden gems, with each recommendation a key to unlocking a new adventure. The stories were not just about the places; they were about connections made, lessons learned, and horizons broadened.

Now, here's the call to action for you, dear reader. If you're a traveler at heart, craving experiences that go beyond the ordinary, YBNB is your portal to the extraordinary. It's not just about finding a place to stay; it's about discovering a home in every corner of the world.

Join the YBNB community and be part of this ever-growing tapestry of travel tales. Whether you're an explorer seeking adventure, a digital nomad in search of a new workspace, or a family looking for a memorable vacation, YBNB has something for everyone. Embrace this chance to step out of your comfort zone, to find comfort in the unknown, and to weave your own travel stories that are worth telling and retelling.

In conclusion, the 2023 YBNB event was more than just a gathering; it was a celebration of the spirit of travel. And now, it's your turn to be a part of this exciting journey. Join YBNB, and let's make every night the best night of your travels. Safe travels and unforgettable adventures await!

TRAVEL |TRIENT PRESS

TRIENT PRESS MAGAZINE FEBRUARY/ MARCH

SYCUAN RESORT

"A Red Carpet Experience Amidst Serenity"

BY M.L. RUSCSAK

In the realm of luxury travel, certain destinations stand apart, offering not just a place to stay but an experience to be cherished. Sycuan Resort is one such gem, a sanctuary of comfort and elegance nestled in the picturesque landscape of San Diego's Dehesa Valley.

As a seasoned traveler and an avid explorer of luxurious retreats, my stay at Sycuan Resort was an experience that resonated with both the serenity of nature and the glamour of a red carpet event. From the moment I arrived, it was evident that Sycuan is a place where every detail is meticulously crafted to ensure an exceptional stay.

TRAVEL |TRIENT PRESS

Imagine stepping into a haven where the hustle of the city fades into a tranquil melody of nature's own. The resort's design harmoniously blends modern luxury with the natural beauty surrounding it, creating an ambiance of peaceful elegance. The rooms are not just accommodations; they are sanctuaries of comfort, outfitted with plush furnishings and state-of-the-art amenities, each offering a panoramic view of the lush valley or the beautifully manicured golf courses.

But what truly sets Sycuan Resort apart is its unparalleled hospitality. The staff's attention to detail and commitment to guest satisfaction is evident in every interaction. They are not just employees; they are artisans of hospitality, ensuring that every aspect of your stay is perfect.

The culinary experience at Sycuan is a journey through diverse flavors and exquisite dining options. From gourmet restaurants to casual dining spots, each meal is a celebration of taste, crafted by chefs who are maestros in their field. Whether you're indulging in a fine dining experience or enjoying a casual meal, the quality of food and service is consistently outstanding.

TRIENT PRESS MAGAZINE   FEBRUARY/ MARCH

Sycuan's ability to host red carpet events is a spectacle of its own. The resort transforms into a dazzling stage, where elegance and excitement blend seamlessly. The events are meticulously organized, each element reflecting the resort's commitment to excellence. As a guest, you're not just attending an event; you're part of an exclusive experience, a celebration of luxury and style.

For those seeking relaxation, the resort's spa is a sanctuary of rejuvenation. The treatments are more than just procedures; they are rituals of relaxation, designed to soothe your body and mind. The serene ambiance of the spa, combined with the expertise of the therapists, makes each visit a rejuvenating escape.

In conclusion, my stay at Sycuan Resort was an embodiment of luxury and serenity. It's a place where the cares of the world melt away, leaving you in a state of blissful relaxation. Whether you're seeking a peaceful getaway, a luxurious retreat, or a venue for a glamorous event, Sycuan Resort exceeds expectations on every level.

I wholeheartedly recommend Sycuan Resort for anyone looking for an exceptional travel experience. It's not just a resort; it's a journey into the heart of luxury and tranquility. Discover Sycuan Resort – where every stay is a red carpet experience.

TRAVEL |TRIENT PRESS

Exploring "The Other Side of San Diego": A Quirky Guide to Fun-Filled Adventures

BY: KRISTINA WENZL-FIGUEROA

TRAVEL | TRIENT PRESS

San Diego

Nestled along the sun-kissed coast of Southern California lies a city bursting with vibrant culture, stunning landscapes, and a plethora of activities waiting to be explored. While San Diego is renowned for its beautiful beaches and iconic attractions like the San Diego Zoo and SeaWorld, there's a lesser-known side to this city that beckons to be discovered. Step off the beaten path and delve into the quirky and unconventional side of San Diego for an unforgettable adventure unlike any other.

TRIENT PRESS MAGAZINE FEBRUARY/ MARCH

UNLEASH YOUR INNER CHILD AT COIN-OP GAME ROOM

Tucked away in the bustling neighborhood of North Park, Coin-Op Game Room is a haven for nostalgia seekers and arcade enthusiasts alike. Step inside this retro-inspired bar and arcade, where the flashing lights of vintage pinball machines and the sound of classic arcade games fill the air. Sip on craft cocktails or local brews as you challenge your friends to a game of Pac-Man or Street Fighter. With its laid-back ambiance and extensive selection of games, Coin-Op offers a unique twist on traditional nightlife activities.

TRAVEL | TRIENT PRESS

TRIENT PRESS MAGAZINE   FEBRUARY/ MARCH

EMBARK ON A CULINARY ADVENTURE AT LIBERTY PUBLIC MARKET:

Foodies rejoice at Liberty Public Market, located in the heart of San Diego's historic Liberty Station. This bustling marketplace brings together a diverse array of local vendors, artisans, and chefs, offering everything from artisanal cheeses and gourmet chocolates to freshly shucked oysters and craft cocktails. Wander through the maze of stalls, sampling delectable treats and soaking in the lively atmosphere. Don't miss the chance to indulge in a savory lobster roll from Wicked Maine Lobster or satisfy your sweet tooth with a decadent ice cream sandwich from Scooped by MooTime Creamery.

TRAVEL | TRIENT PRESS

TRIENT PRESS MAGAZINE FEBRUARY/ MARCH

DISCOVER UNDERWATER WONDERS AT BIRCH AQUARIUM

While many visitors flock to San Diego's famous beaches, few venture beneath the surface to explore the fascinating world of marine life. Located in La Jolla overlooking the Pacific Ocean, Birch Aquarium offers a captivating glimpse into the wonders of the sea.

Marvel at vibrant coral reefs, graceful seahorses, and elusive sharks as you wander through the aquarium's interactive exhibits. Dive deeper into ocean conservation efforts with hands-on activities and educational programs suitable for all ages. From mesmerizing jellyfish displays to breathtaking panoramic views of the coast, Birch Aquarium promises an unforgettable aquatic adventure.

TRAVEL | TRIENT PRESS

TRIENT PRESS MAGAZINE　　　　　　　　FEBRUARY/ MARCH

CHANNEL YOUR INNER ARTIST AT BALBOA PARK'S SPANISH VILLAGE ART CENTER:

Step into a world of creativity and inspiration at the Spanish Village Art Center, nestled within the sprawling grounds of Balboa Park. This colorful enclave showcases the works of over 200 local artists, ranging from painters and sculptors to jewelry makers and ceramicists. Stroll through the charming cobblestone pathways lined with vibrant studios and galleries, where you can watch artists at work and purchase one-of-a-kind pieces to take home as souvenirs. Immerse yourself in San Diego's thriving arts scene and unleash your own creativity with hands-on workshops and classes offered by resident artists

TRAVEL |TRIENT PRESS

TRIENT PRESS MAGAZINE   FEBRUARY/ MARCH

UNWIND IN NATURE AT SUNSET CLIFFS NATURAL PARK:

For those seeking solace amidst San Diego's bustling urban landscape, Sunset Cliffs Natural Park offers a serene escape to nature's beauty. Perched atop rugged coastal cliffs overlooking the Pacific Ocean, this breathtaking park boasts panoramic views of the horizon illuminated by the golden hues of sunset.

Take a leisurely stroll along the winding pathways, breathe in the salty sea air, and listen to the soothing sounds of crashing waves below. Whether you're seeking solitude or simply savoring the moment with loved ones, Sunset Cliffs provides the perfect backdrop for relaxation and reflection.

As you wander off the beaten path and explore "The Other Side of San Diego," you'll discover a city brimming with hidden gems and offbeat adventures waiting to be uncovered. From retro arcade games and culinary delights to artistic enclaves and natural wonders, San Diego offers a diverse array of experiences sure to delight and inspire visitors of all ages. So, pack your sense of curiosity and embark on a journey to uncover the unexpected in America's Finest City.

TRAVEL |TRIENT PRESS

Navigating the World: A Deaf Traveler's Perspective

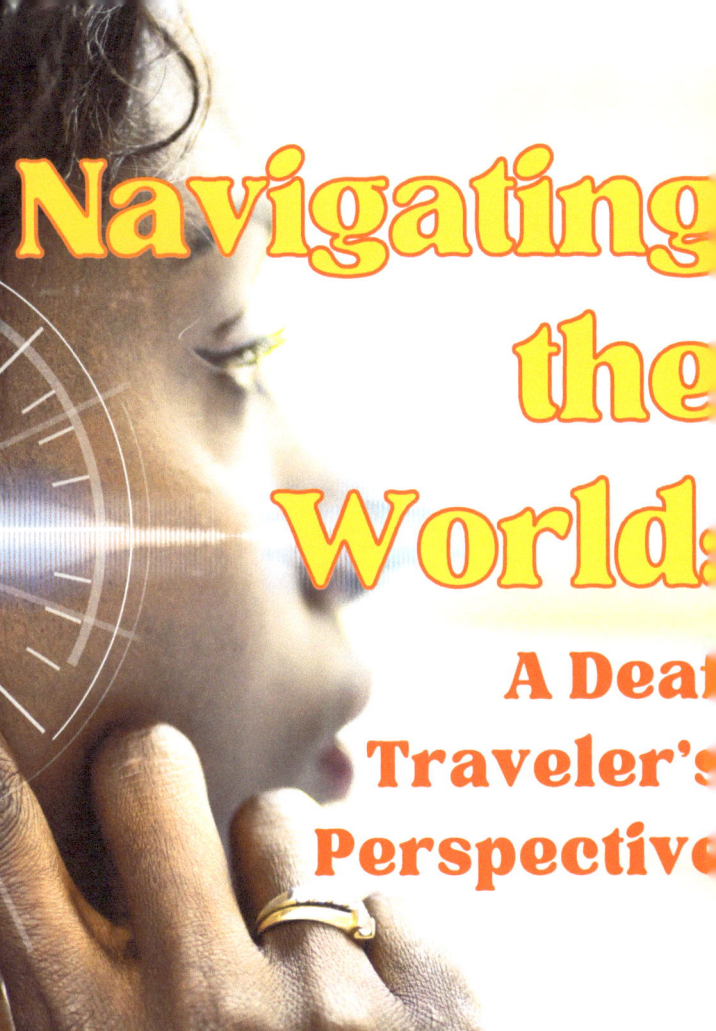

BY KRISTINA WENZL-FIGUEROA

"Traveling alongside my deaf friend, I've come to appreciate the rich tapestry of experiences beyond just what we hear. Our journey isn't about the sounds around us, but about the colorful mosaic of visuals, vibrations, and shared connections that unfold with each new adventure. In embracing this unique perspective, we discover the true essence of travel: a boundless world of inclusivity, empathy, and shared discovery."

In a world where travel writing often highlights the sights, sounds, and flavors of destinations, there's an overlooked perspective that deserves its own spotlight: the journey of a deaf traveler. Traveling with a hearing impairment brings unique challenges and enriching experiences that seldom find their way into mainstream narratives. In this feature, we delve into the world of deaf travel, exploring both the obstacles faced and the vibrant tapestry of connections, cultures, and communication that define it.

TRAVEL | TRIENT PRESS

TRIENT PRESS MAGAZINE   FEBRUARY/ MARCH

A DIFFERENT SOUNDSCAPE

For deaf travelers, the auditory landscape of a destination presents an entirely different experience. While bustling markets, roaring waterfalls, and the buzz of city streets are the quintessential sounds of travel, they paint only a fraction of the picture for those who navigate the world without hearing. Instead, deaf travelers perceive the world through a mosaic of visuals, vibrations, and interactions.

Take, for example, the majesty of Niagara Falls. While many revel in its thunderous roar, a deaf traveler might find solace in the rhythmic vibrations of the water, feeling its power resonate through the ground beneath their feet. Similarly, the cacophony of a bustling bazaar transforms into a symphony of colors and gestures, each telling a story that transcends language barriers.

BRIDGING THE COMMUNICATION GAP

Communication is the cornerstone of travel, yet for deaf individuals, traditional methods such a verbal dialogue often prove inaccessible. However, this barrier fosters creativity and innovation in communication, leading to a rich tapestry of interactions that transcend spoken language.
Sign language becomes a universal bridge, allowing deaf travelers to connect with locals and fellow travelers alike. Whether through American Sign Language (ASL), British Sign Language (BSL), or regional variants, sign language serves as a conduit for shared experiences, laughter, and understanding. Additionally, technology plays a pivotal role in leveling the communication playing field. From mobile apps that facilitate real-time text translation to video relay services that enable phone conversations through sign language interpreters, technology empowers deaf travelers to engage with the world on their terms.

TRAVEL |TRIENT PRESS

TRIENT PRESS MAGAZINE

CULTIVATING EMPATHY AND UNDERSTANDING

Traveling as a deaf individual offers more than just a change of scenery; it fosters empathy, understanding, and appreciation for diversity. Every interaction becomes an opportunity to bridge the gap between the hearing and deaf worlds, dispelling misconceptions and fostering meaningful connections.

Deaf travelers often find themselves at the forefront of cultural exchange, offering insights into the deaf experience and challenging societal norms along the way. Through their journeys, they dismantle barriers, reshape perceptions, and pave the way for a more inclusive travel landscape.

EMBRACING THE JOURNEY

While the path of a deaf traveler may be paved with obstacles, it is also illuminated by moments of profound beauty, connection, and discovery. From scaling towering peaks to wandering ancient alleyways, each step is a testament to the resilience and spirit of exploration that transcends language and hearing.

As we venture into a world that is as diverse as it is interconnected, let us not forget the myriad perspectives that enrich our collective journey. Through the eyes of a deaf traveler, we gain a deeper appreciation for the boundless tapestry of human experience that unites us all.

In the end, perhaps the true essence of travel lies not in the destination, but in the connections we forge along the way—connections that transcend barriers of language, culture, and hearing, reminding us that in the vast mosaic of humanity, there is beauty in every hue. Let us not overlook the perspectives of deaf travelers, which highlight the challenges they face and the unique experiences they bring to the world of travel. Through their journeys we gain a deeper understanding of the power of communication and how far a little understanding can go when seeing others navigate the experiences we share, who are different than us.

So, let us embark on this journey together, embracing the richness of diversity and the power of empathy as we navigate the world, one step at a time.

TRAVEL | TRIENT PRESS

UNVEILING THE WORLD OF DARK TOURISM:

EXPLORING THE UNCONVENTIONAL SIDE OF TRAVEL

BY: KRISTINA WENZL-FIGUEROA

In the bustling realm of travel, where Instagram-worthy destinations and luxury resorts often steal the spotlight, there exists a niche that ventures beyond the conventional. It's a realm where history's darkest chapters intertwine with curiosity, creating an unconventional yet profoundly enlightening form of exploration. Welcome to the world of Dark Tourism – a facet of travel that sheds light on the obscure, the macabre, and the hauntingly captivating aspects of human history.

What is Dark Tourism?

Dark Tourism, often referred to as thanatourism, revolves around visiting places associated with death, tragedy, or suffering. From former concentration camps to abandoned ghost towns, from disaster sites to eerie catacombs, these destinations offer travelers a unique perspective on the human experience, confronting them with the complexities of our collective past.

BEYOND THE SURFACE: UNDERSTANDING THE APPEAL

While Dark Tourism might seem morbid at first glance, its allure lies in its ability to provoke thought, evoke empathy, and foster a deeper understanding of the world we inhabit. It's not merely about seeking thrills in the macabre; rather, it's an endeavor to comprehend the narratives woven into the fabric of these destinations.

For some, visiting sites of historical significance serves as a form of remembrance – a way to honor the lives lost and acknowledge the events that shaped our present. For others, it's a means of confronting mortality and gaining perspective on the transient nature of human existence. Whatever the motivation, Dark Tourism offers a profound journey into the heart of human resilience and the enduring quest for meaning amidst adversity.

"Dark tourism isn't about chasing ghosts; it's about illuminating the shadows of our collective history to better understand the light of our shared humanity."

TRAVEL | TRIENT PRESS

Exploring darkness unveils the light of empathy in our shared history

EXPLORING THE UNCONVENTIONAL

One of the most intriguing aspects of Dark Tourism is its sheer diversity. From the haunting relics of Chernobyl's nuclear disaster to the somber corridors of Auschwitz-Birkenau, each destination offers a unique lens through which to view history.

In Cambodia, the Killing Fields stand as a harrowing testament to the atrocities committed during the Khmer Rouge regime. Here, visitors bear witness to mass graves and haunting memorials, grappling with the unfathomable suffering endured by the Cambodian people.

Meanwhile, in Japan, the Aokigahara Forest – known as the "Suicide Forest" – draws curious travelers and psychologists alike. Amidst the dense foliage lie the silent remnants of those who chose this ethereal landscape as their final resting place, sparking conversations about mental health and societal pressures

TRAVEL | TRIENT PRESS

THE ETHICAL DILEMMA

While Dark Tourism offers invaluable insights, it also raises ethical questions regarding commodification, voyeurism, and respect for the deceased. Balancing the educational value of these experiences with the need for sensitivity and reverence is paramount in ensuring that visitors engage with these sites responsibly.

Furthermore, the impact of tourism on fragile ecosystems and local communities must be carefully considered. Sustainable practices and community engagement initiatives can mitigate the negative consequences of increased visitor traffic, preserving these sites for future generations to learn from and reflect upon.

EMBRACING THE SHADOWS:

In a world where glossy brochures and pristine beaches dominate the travel industry, Dark Tourism offers a compelling alternative – one that challenges our preconceptions, prompts introspection, and fosters empathy. It's a journey into the shadows, where the echoes of the past resonate with profound significance, reminding us of our shared humanity and the enduring lessons of history.

So, the next time you plan your travels, consider veering off the beaten path and delving into the realm of Dark Tourism. Amidst the darkness, you may just discover a newfound appreciation for the light that guides us forward.

"Dark tourism revealed hidden stories, connecting me deeply to our shared history."

Crab Macaroni & Cheese

INGREDIENTS

- Salt- for boiling pasta
- 2 C. macaroni
- 3 TB butter
- 1 1/2 tablespoon flour
- 1 C. milk
- 1 C. cheddar, grated
- 1/2 C. gruyere, grated
- 1 pinch of nutmeg (whole and grated or ground)
- ~1 C. CLEANED, dried crab

SIMPLE RECIPE

DIRECTIONS

1. Preheat oven grill to 375 degrees Fahrenheit.

2. Bring a saucepan of salted water to the boil.

3. Cook the pasta as per packet instructions, make the sauce in the meantime, draining the pasta when it cooked.

4. To create the cheese sauce, first make a roux by melting the butter on a low heat in a saucepan, then slowly whisk in the flour to form a paste.

5. Cook and stir for 5 minutes.

6. Add a small amount of milk and leave to boil.

7. Once the mixture is boiling, reduce the heat to medium and slowly add the rest of the milk, whisking vigorously for about 10-15 minutes- until the mixture is a smooth non-lumpy consistency.

8. Add in most of the grated cheddar and gruyere, grate in or add some ground nutmeg and stir continuously until the cheese has melted.

9. Add the cooked pasta to the sauce and gently stir, before folding in the crabmeat.

10. Spoon into small dishes, sprinkle on the remaining cheese and place under the grill until the top layer of cheese is golden brown and the pasta is heated through fully.

11. Remove the mac and cheese dishes from the grill and plate up with the Arugula Salad *below

Adjustments:
- Add parmesan as well, if you have any in the fridge to use up.
- An Arugula Salad with lemon juice, olive oil and salt makes for a complimentary side dish-it cuts right through the rich sauce.

TRAVEL |TRIENT PRESS

SIMPLE RECIPE

Arugula Spring Salad ★★★★☆

A perfect companion to any rich main course. This rocket salad (arugula leaf) with pear, (walnuts & feta), Parmesan and lemon maple dressing is super simple and quick to make and makes for a nutritious side dish.

INGREDIENTS

- 4 CUPS ROCKET LEAVES WASHED AND DRIED
- 1 CUP GRATED PARMESAN CHEESE AGED PARMESAN IS BEST
- 1 CUP PEAR 1/2 OF LARGE PEAR, THINLY SLICED
- JUICE OF 1/2 LARGE LEMON ABOUT 2 TABLESPOONS
- 2 TABLESPOON OLIVE OIL
- 2 TEASPOONS MAPLE SYRUP
- HANDFUL OF WALNUTS OR FETA CHEESE (OPT)
- A GOOD PINCH OF SEA SALT AND PEPPER

DIRECTIONS

- If needed, wash and dry the rocket leaves and add them to a big salad bowl.
- Shave or grate Parmesan cheese over the top, about a cup.
- Slice half a pear into thin little strips or cubes.
- Add the dressing ingredients straight over the top just before serving: lemon juice, maple syrup, olive oil, sea salt and pepper.
- Toss everything together and serve.
- Add walnuts (roasted is optional) & feta

TRAVEL |TRIENT PRESS

www.ingramcontent.com/pod-product-compliance
Ingram Content Group UK Ltd.
Pitfield, Milton Keynes, MK11 3LW, UK
UKHW060138240426
12048UKWH00003B/87